@work

Student's Book

with additional material
by James Greenan

Richmond

Contents

More
practice = more practice available on the digital and print Workbook

My world of work

A day in the life of ...

| 8 a.m. | noon | 7 p.m. | 10 p.m. |

Start up

1 Look at the pictures and discuss the questions with a partner.

1 What time of day do you prefer?
2 When do you work best?
3 When are you at your least effective?
4 What do you normally do at each of the times of day?
5 What are you doing this week that's different from other weeks?

Reading

2 Read the text and complete the sentences.

1 When working, Jourdan normally stays in .... , but this week, she .... at her mum's.
2 When she isn't doing modelling shows, she sometimes ....
3 She still .... in normal stores and enjoys eating ....
4 She .... to lots of model parties.

The life of a supermodel

Jourdan Dunn, from west London, was shopping for sunglasses when she was spotted by a scout from the agency that discovered Kate Moss.

But modelling isn't always as glamorous as some people think. Normally, Jourdan stays in models' apartments when she's on tour, but she doesn't enjoy it. 'I hate staying in models' apartments. Most models usually have their mums running around looking after them, so the house is a mess. I'm a clean person so it's hard to cope.' But this week is London Fashion Week and she's staying at home, eating home-cooked food and watching the British soap opera *EastEnders*.

Dunn doesn't do modelling just for fun – she's a career woman with a busy schedule. After three 5.00 a.m. starts during London Fashion Week, she's then flying to Milan for the next round of shows. New York, London, Milan and Paris fashion weeks all follow on from one another, so it's a non-stop round of castings, auditions and catwalk shows. After

that comes to an end, she's doing shoots for magazines and campaigns, and is modelling in one-off shows.

While many things have changed for Dunn, she has changed few lifestyle habits since starting modelling; she still shops on the high street, wears trainers rather than high heels, and eats junk food.

Although Dunn's living in the spotlight at the moment, she doesn't let success go to her head, and says she still hangs out with the same friends rather than other models. As for the glamorous after-parties, they're all full of old people, 'I'm not really into after-parties. I feel like I'll be with a bunch of people not my age.'

reuters.com ©Thomson Reuters 2008

3 Read the text again. What does she do regularly and what's she doing this week? What difference is there in the verb form used?

Grammar

More practice

4 Look at the table. Match the rules with the example sentence.

Present simple		
1 A long-term activity	**a**	She doesn't let success go to her head.
2 A long-term state	**b**	Normally Jourdan stays in a models' apartment.
3 A regular activity	**c**	She does photo shoots for magazines.

Present continuous		
1 A temporary activity	**a**	She's then flying to Milan.
2 A future arrangement	**b**	She's staying with her mother.
3 An action happening at the moment of speaking	**c**	She's eating lunch as we speak.

〉〉〉GRAMMAR REFERENCE PAGE 102

5 Complete the sentences with the correct form of the present simple or present continuous.

1 I .... (work) on this project all this week.
2 They .... (visit) clients every Monday.
3 He .... (live) a five-minute walk away from work.
4 We .... (take) a holiday next week.
5 Can I call you back in a minute? I .... (eat) my lunch.

Listening

6 You're going to listen to John, a cycle courier. Look at the things he does. Which ones do you think he does regularly and which are just temporary?

1 cycle 50 to 100 miles ....
2 work 9.00 to 5.00 ....
3 not take a lunch break ....
4 carry files and envelopes ....
5 carry clothes ....
6 earn £200 per week ....

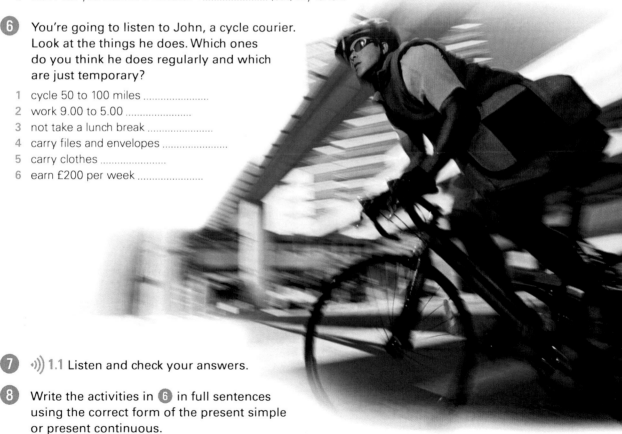

7 ᵒ))) 1.1 Listen and check your answers.

8 Write the activities in **6** in full sentences using the correct form of the present simple or present continuous.

John cycles 50 to 100 miles every day.

Speaking

9 Write down six things you regularly do in your job. Tell your partner which ones you enjoy the most and the least.

10 Think about a project or something you're doing at the moment that's short-term or not regular work. Tell a partner what's involved and what you like and dislike about it.

Start up ① Match the departments 1–6 with their functions a–f.

Department	This department ...
1 Accounts	a is in charge of buying products and services for a company.
2 Human Resources	b is in charge of computer hardware and software.
3 IT	c makes the things a company sells.
4 Office Services	d provides administrative support.
5 Production	e is in charge of financial matters.
6 Purchasing	f runs staff training and development, and is responsible for recruiting and dismissing staff.

② Discuss the questions with a partner.

1 Which departments from ① do you have in your company?

2 What other departments do you have?

3 Which department do you work in?

Listening ③ ◁)) 1.2 Listen to Jan describing his company, FIB Manufacturing. Complete the chart.

.... 1
Aksel Lindberg

| Director of .... 2 Aleksej Lindström | Director of marketing .... 3 | Director of manufacturing Taka Akita | Director of .... 4 Domar Lindgren | Director of human resources Oli Richards |

line manager – the manager directly responsible for someone
hierarchy – a system or organisation that has many levels from the lowest to the highest

| Industrial engineering manager Edda Lundberg | .... 5 manager Tatsuki Sano | .... 6 manager Rachel Skinner |
| .... 7 manager Jan Bergstrom | .... 8 manager Richard Smith | .... 9 manager Yumi Nohara |

④ Does your company have a clear and simple structure? Is there a strong, traditional hierarchy like the one in ③?

Reading ⑤ Read the text about Oticon. How is its hierarchical structure different from a traditional one?

The Danish company Oticon is the second largest producer of hearing aids in the world. It employs about 4,500 people worldwide and around 1,200 in Denmark. In the 1980s, competition became much stronger for Oticon. In 1988, Lars Kolind became the new chief executive and in 1990, he decided that a new strategy was needed. Kolind decided to change how the company was structured and organised.

Product development was organised around projects. The management team appointed a project leader who recruited people to do the work. Employees could choose to work on any project, or not, as long as their current project leader agreed. Most employees previously had a single skill, but now required at least three specialities: one skill was based on a professional qualification and the other skills were unrelated, such as customer support or advertising. This allowed the company to respond more quickly and to use skills fully.

The only part of the old hierarchy that still remains is the ten-person management team. There are no job titles; people do whatever they think is right at the time. With no departments, people don't protect local interests and it's easier to cope with changes in workloads. The company has values such as 'an assumption that we only employ adults (who can be expected to behave responsibly)' and 'an assumption that staff want to know what and why they're doing it'. Oticon believes that if the processes are defined clearly, then the company can be more flexible. Kolind refers to this as 'managed chaos'.

6 Read the text again and match the two parts of the sentences.

1	The management team are in charge	a	their own workloads.
2	Employees report to	b	responsibility.
3	Employees are responsible for	c	the project leader.
4	The hierarchy helps the company deal with	d	a department.
5	People don't work for	e	changes in workloads.
6	Employees are given	f	of project leaders.

7 Work in pairs. Write the advantages in the correct column.

a It gives employees more responsibility in the organisation.
b Employees become specialists.
c It improves coordination and speed of communication.
d Employees look out for the best interests of their department.
e There's an easier decision-making process among employees.
f It reduces an organisation's budget costs.
g Opportunities for promotion motivate employees to perform well.

Flat hierarchy	Traditional hierarchy

8 Compare your ideas with another pair.

Vocabulary **9** You're going to listen to Jan describing his role in FIB. Before you listen, complete the sentences with words from the box.

| in charge of   look after   report to   responsible for   work alongside |
| work for   work in |

More practice

1 I _work for_ FIB Manufacturing.
2 I'm a shift manager and .... the main factory.
3 I .... two other shift managers.
4 I .... Taksuki Sano, the factory manager.
5 I'm .... twenty production assistants.
6 It's my responsibility to .... all the machinery and factory staff.
7 We have targets to meet each day and I'm .... my team meeting these targets.

10))) 1.3 Listen and check.

Speaking **11** Work with a partner. Use the verbs and prepositions from **9** to describe your job.

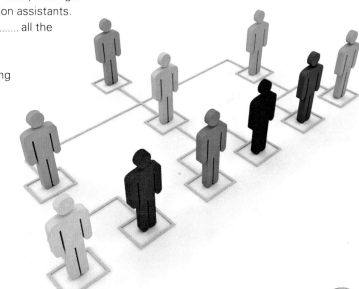

Start up **1** Tell a partner about when you do the following things in English. Who's it to/with? What's it usually about?

1 have a meeting	3 make a phone call
2 send an email	4 watch a film

Reading **2** Read the text about phoning in English and complete the sentences.

1 Telephoning can be an advantage because ....

2 The best way to make your phone call successful is ....

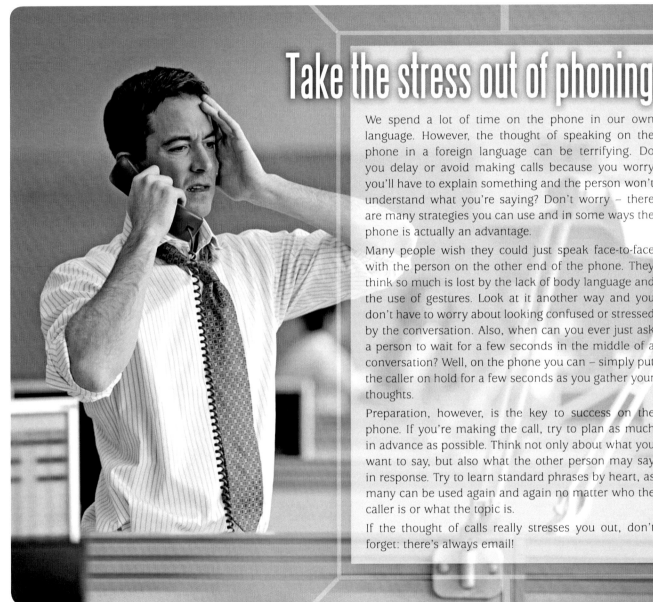

Take the stress out of phoning

We spend a lot of time on the phone in our own language. However, the thought of speaking on the phone in a foreign language can be terrifying. Do you delay or avoid making calls because you worry you'll have to explain something and the person won't understand what you're saying? Don't worry – there are many strategies you can use and in some ways the phone is actually an advantage.

Many people wish they could just speak face-to-face with the person on the other end of the phone. They think so much is lost by the lack of body language and the use of gestures. Look at it another way and you don't have to worry about looking confused or stressed by the conversation. Also, when can you ever just ask a person to wait for a few seconds in the middle of a conversation? Well, on the phone you can – simply put the caller on hold for a few seconds as you gather your thoughts.

Preparation, however, is the key to success on the phone. If you're making the call, try to plan as much in advance as possible. Think not only about what you want to say, but also what the other person may say in response. Try to learn standard phrases by heart, as many can be used again and again no matter who the caller is or what the topic is.

If the thought of calls really stresses you out, don't forget: there's always email!

3 Read the text again and answer the questions.

1 How do people sometimes feel talking on the phone in another language?

2 What do people prefer to the phone?

3 What other things help face-to-face communication?

4 What can you do on the phone that you can't do face-to-face?

5 What three things should you do before a call?

4 Tell a partner whether you agree with the ideas in the text or not. Try to add more strategies for making calls in English.

Listening ⑤ ·))) **1.4** Listen to three phone calls. Why can't they speak to the person they need to speak to?

1 ....   3 ....
2 ....

⑥ Work with a partner. Complete each useful telephone phrase with the number of words in brackets.

1 Can I *ask who's* (2) calling?
2 Can you .... (2) a moment?
3 Can I .... (1) a message?
4 Can you .... (2) to call me back?
5 Can you .... (2) your name again, please?
6 Can you .... (2) again, please?

⑦ ·))) **1.5** Listen to a call and check your answers.

Say it right ⑧ ·))) **1.6** Listen to the questions from ⑥ being said in two different ways. Decide which question sounds more polite in each case. Write P for polite and R for rude for each one.

| 1 a ☐ b ☐ | 3 a ☐ b ☐ | 5 a ☐ b ☐ |
| 2 a ☐ b ☐ | 4 a ☐ b ☐ | 6 a ☐ b ☐ |

⑨ Listen again and practise the polite intonation.

Listening ⑩ Match parts of the sentence from each column to make different ways to check information.

1 Is that	your number	one *L* in the middle or two?
2 Did you say	say	you're calling from?
3 I'm sorry,	I didn't catch	is 972 8773?
4 Where did you	with	please?
5 Could you	spell it,	or *B* for Bertie?
6 Is that *P*	for Paul	your name.

⑪ ·))) **1.7** Listen to two calls and check your answers to ⑩.

⑫ Listen again. Why is each person calling?

1 ....   2 ....

⑬ ·))) **1.8** Listen to the first call being returned.

1 What's the problem?
2 Are there spellings of names for different genders which people easily confuse in your native language?

⑭ Compare the message from the second call with the audioscript on page 116. What problem will Connie have?

Connie,
Could you ring Andrew Newton about the
next course coming up on 01568 926669?
Laura

Speaking ⑮ Work with a partner. Practise leaving and taking messages over the phone. Student A, look at the information below. Student B, look at page 96.

• You work for Circo on their reception. Answer the phone.
• Try to contact the person your partner wants to speak to.
• The person isn't there. Ask about taking a message.

Richmond Design Solutions, a graphic design company, has recently hired Fredrik Sandgren to take charge of their administration department. The management team was really impressed with his ideas for changing the structure of the department.

1))) **1.9** Listen to a description of how the department is currently organised and complete the information that follows.

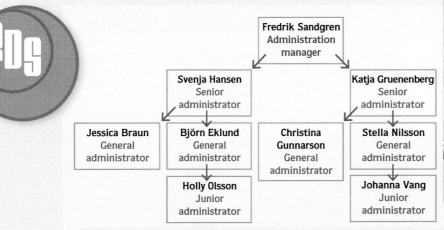

Fredrik Sandgren
Administration manager

Svenja Hansen Senior administrator

Katja Gruenenberg Senior administrator

Jessica Braun General administrator

Björn Eklund General administrator

Christina Gunnarson General administrator

Stella Nilsson General administrator

Holly Olsson Junior administrator

Johanna Vang Junior administrator

Senior administrators look after ....[1] and deal with legal contracts. They ....[2] admin services to the ....[3] design project managers. General administrators: Jessica and Björn are ....[4] meeting room bookings, catering, and business trip ....[5]. Christina and Stella deal with the ....[6] for the ten designers on the design team. Junior administrators answer all ....[7] and email enquiries, deal with ....[8] and order stationery.

2))) **1.10** Listen to part of the interview Fredrik had. Complete the table with his plans for the department.

Roles	He plans for employees to have no ....[1] or ....[2].
Training	In the new system, employees will need ....[3].
Managing workload	Fredrik thinks the biggest advantage of his plan is ....[4].
Working methods	People won't have set tasks to do, ...[5] will have tasks to do.

3 Read the text about how the department is currently organised. What problems do you think the new manager might have with his ideas for changes?

Richmond Design Solutions has a very strong hierarchy and line of command. It's very clear who's in charge of each department and it's their role to allocate tasks to members of staff. When the company hires new staff, they do so with a specific job in mind and as a result, they hire people with very clear skills, experience and expertise in these areas. The company operates a flexible working schedule with core hours from 10.00 to 3.00. Once staff have completed their work, they often leave early or arrive late the next day. The conditions for workers in the company are very good. There's a good holiday allowance, salary and pension fund. Once people start working in the company, they tend to stay there for a very long time. The company's very proud of its staff retention, but a little frustrated by the lack of dynamism in the company.

4 ◈))) **1.11** Listen to a conversation over lunch. Why is each person not happy?

Björn	Christina	Jessica

5 Fredrik has reorganised his department. Look at the new organigram and make a list of some problems it could cause. Discuss your ideas with a partner.

Fredrik Sandgren
Administration
manager
↓

Svenja Hansen, Katja Gruenenberg, Jessica Braun, Björn Eklund, Christina Gunnarson, Stella Nilsson, Holly Olsson, Johanna Vang
Administration team

Possible problems
Staff unhappy with their salary if they're given more responsibility but no more money
....
....
....
....
....

6 ◈))) **1.12** Listen to a conversation between Fredrik and his manager, Karin. Answer the questions.

1 What problems do the designers have with the new system?
2 Why are the key customers unhappy?
3 What are Svenja and Katja unhappy about?
4 What are Holly and Johanna asking for? Why?
5 What does Karin think Fredrik should do?

7 Karin has suggested that if Fredrik wants to keep the flat hierarchy, he should define roles and responsibilities clearly. Look at her suggestions and compare them with the old organigram in ①. Which is better and why? Discuss your ideas with a partner.

Fredrik Sandgren
Administration
manager
↓

Svenja Hansen, Katja Gruenenberg, Jessica Braun, Björn Eklund, Christina Gunnarson, Stella Nilsson, Holly Olsson, Johanna Vang
Administration team

All team members now have the following responsibilities: answer phone calls, deal with new email enquiries, organise meetings, book catering, arrange business trips.
Other responsibilities are divided as follows.
Svenja: Responsible for Key Customer 1 and legal contracts.
Katja: Responsible for Key Customer 2 and legal contracts.
Jessica and Björn: Responsible for Key Customer 1 when Svenja is busy. Deal with admin for 4 design project managers.
Christina and Stella: Responsible for Key Customer 2 when Katja is busy. Deal with admin for 4 design project managers.
Holly and Johanna: Deal with admin for 10 designers and assist other members of admin team where necessary.

Motivation

Think success

Start up

1 Look at the pictures and discuss the questions with a partner.

1 What kinds of books do you like reading?
2 What was the last book you read? Did you enjoy reading it?
3 Do you ever read books related to your job or career?
4 Have you ever read a self-help book?

Reading

2 Read the text and complete the table.

Number	Event
250,000 +	*The number of self-help and personal success books on Amazon*
1883	
13	
1908	
500	
30 million	

THINK AND GROW RICH

THIS BOOK COULD BE WORTH A MILLION DOLLARS TO YOU.

THINK & GROW RICH

BY NAPOLEON HILL

A search for self-help or personal success books on Amazon shows a quarter of a million hits. Some individual titles sell tens of millions of copies worldwide, but where and when did this publishing phenomenon start?

Napoleon Hill is considered to be one of the first writers of a self-help book. An American author, he was born in 1883 in the town of Pound, south-west of Virginia. He started work at the age of thirteen on a newspaper. He used the money he earned from writing to pay to go to Law School, but he left for financial reasons.

In 1908, he was writing a series of articles about famous and successful men. One of the men he met was Andrew Carnegie. At the time, Carnegie was one of the most powerful men in the world. Carnegie believed he could create an easy-to-understand formula for success by interviewing the richest and most successful people in the world. He commissioned Hill to interview over 500 successful people to discover the secret of their success. Hill interviewed many of the most famous people of the time, including Thomas Edison, Alexander Graham Bell, Henry Ford and Theodore Roosevelt.

Hill and Carnegie published the multi-volume course called *The Law of Success*. Hill's most famous book was called *Think and Grow Rich*, but the book doesn't actually offer any straight ideas. He felt that readers needed to discover it for themselves and that the main reason most people were not successful was that they didn't have any firm beliefs. He challenged readers to think about the question 'What do I truly believe in?'

Think and Grow Rich is still Napoleon Hill's bestselling book, having sold over 30 million copies.

3 These verbs all appear in the past simple in the text. Write the past simple form and then check your answers with the text.

Paragraph 2 – be born, start, leave
Paragraph 3 – meet, believe, commission, interview
Paragraph 4 – publish, feel, challenge

Grammar

4 Complete the rules about past simple use.

> **Past simple**
>
> We use the past simple to talk about completed actions and events.
> The form of the past simple is the same for all persons, except the verb *be* which uses .... with *I/he/she/it* and .... with *you/we/they*.
> Regular verbs end in *-ed,* but many verbs are irregular.

>>> GRAMMAR REFERENCE PAGE 104

5 Read the text in **6** quickly and complete the sentences.

1 Andrew Carnegie lived in .... and America.
2 He made money from the .... industry.
3 He built many .... in the USA, UK and Canada.
4 He wanted to give the Philippines .... to stop the USA buying it.

More practice

6 Complete the text about Andrew Carnegie with the past simple form of the verbs in brackets.

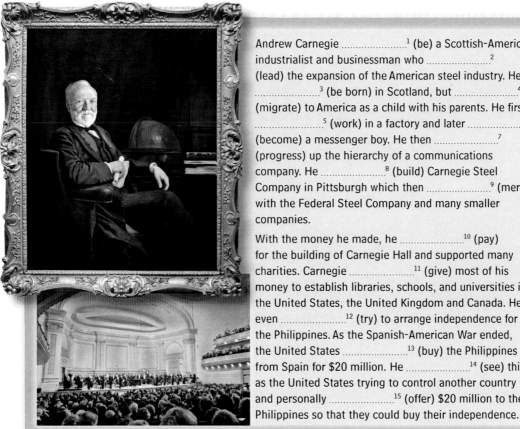

Andrew Carnegie ....[1] (be) a Scottish-American industrialist and businessman who ....[2] (lead) the expansion of the American steel industry. He ....[3] (be born) in Scotland, but ....[4] (migrate) to America as a child with his parents. He first ....[5] (work) in a factory and later ....[6] (become) a messenger boy. He then ....[7] (progress) up the hierarchy of a communications company. He ....[8] (build) Carnegie Steel Company in Pittsburgh which then ....[9] (merge) with the Federal Steel Company and many smaller companies.

With the money he made, he ....[10] (pay) for the building of Carnegie Hall and supported many charities. Carnegie ....[11] (give) most of his money to establish libraries, schools, and universities in the United States, the United Kingdom and Canada. He even ....[12] (try) to arrange independence for the Philippines. As the Spanish-American War ended, the United States ....[13] (buy) the Philippines from Spain for $20 million. He ....[14] (see) this as the United States trying to control another country and personally ....[15] (offer) $20 million to the Philippines so that they could buy their independence.

Speaking

7 Think of five succesful events in your life and write sentences using the past simple to describe when these happened.

8 Tell your partner about these successes and the reasons for them.

13

Start up

1 Work with a partner. Put what motivates you in order of importance.

> achievement   money   praise   security   status

most important ➡ **least important**

2 Add any other ideas you have to the chart.

3 List three things that would make you quit a job. Show them to a partner and discuss the reasons why.

Reading

4 You're going to read a survey about employee job satisfaction. Before you read, try to predict the following:

1 What percentage of people are dissatisfied with their job?
2 What percentage plan to leave their current job?
3 What's the main reason for job dissatisfaction?

5 Read the text and check your predictions.

Employee job satisfaction **is low**, motivation to leave **is lower**

Accenture recently conducted a new global study to learn more about job satisfaction for men and women. While the study revealed similar results for both men and women, those results weren't something companies should be proud of.

Accenture surveyed 3,400 professionals in 29 countries and found that less than half were satisfied with their job. However, nearly three out of four respondents weren't planning to leave their company.

What was making employees so unhappy? The Accenture survey revealed the top four reasons for job dissatisfaction as:

- Being underpaid – 47% of women, 44% of men
- Lack of growth opportunities – 36% of women, 32% of men
- Lack of promotion opportunities – 33% of women, 34% of men
- Feeling trapped – 29% of women, 32% of men

When it comes to pay dissatisfaction, the study revealed that older employees were less motivated by pay than younger employees. Nearly three-quarters – 73% – of Generation Y respondents said that pay motivated them, while 67% of Generation X respondents and just 58% of Baby Boomers said the same.

However, when it came to actually asking for a promotion that was likely to bring higher pay with it, the study revealed that men were far more likely to ask for a promotion (39%) than women (28%).

Company leaders need to take a close look at these survey results and make the necessary changes from within to ensure that employees are happy. Not only does job dissatisfaction damage employee performance, but it can damage company performance, too.

6 **Read the text again and answer the questions.**

1 What do the numbers refer to?

36	34	29	73	39

2 Who is pay least important for?
3 Who is more likely to ask for a promotion?
4 Why do companies need to look at these results?

7 **2.1 Listen to three people talking about why they left their job. Match each person with a reason.**

Kerstin

Marco

Sven

1 He/She was working long hours for not much money.
2 His/Her boss was always giving him/her too much work.
3 The customers were always shouting.

8 **Listen again and complete the sentences.**

1 My boss .... (give) me too much work.
2 I just left one day in the middle of a phone call. A person .... (shout) at me on the phone and I just quit on the spot.
3 This time last year, I .... (work) long hours for not much money and .... (find) it very stressful.

Grammar

More practice

Past continuous

a Unfinished or interrupted actions in the past
I was writing an email when the phone rang.

b Actions around a particular time in the past
They were working in a different company this time last year.

c Repeated action in the past
We were getting complaint after complaint after complaint.

The past simple and past continuous are often used together, especially for interrupted actions. The longer action is in the past continuous and the shorter action that interrupts it is in the past simple.

››› GRAMMAR REFERENCE PAGE 105

9 **Choose the correct form of either the past simple or past continuous.**

A day in my worst job

Last Tuesday, I *left/was leaving*[1] my house at 6 o'clock as usual. I *was sitting/sat*[2] on the train when the train driver announced that there would be a one-hour delay. I *tried/was trying*[3] to work on the train, but so many people *were talking/talked*[4] on their mobile phones that I couldn't concentrate. When I *got/was getting*[5] to work, my boss *waited/was waiting*[6] for me in my office. He *complained/was complaining*[7] that I was late and then *gave/was giving*[8] me a huge pile of data to compile a report for lunchtime. I *spent/was spending*[9] the whole morning writing the report, but my phone *rang/was ringing*[10] constantly. Emails *were filling up/filled up*[11] my inbox all morning as well. It was impossible to concentrate. When my boss *came/was coming*[12] into my office at 12.00, he asked why I *wrote/was still writing*[13] the report. When he said I needed to go on a time management course, that was it – I quit!

Speaking

10 **Think about your previous job and discuss the questions with a partner.**

1 What were you doing when you felt the most satisfied at work?
2 What were you doing when you felt the least satisfied at work?
3 What's the worst day you had recently? Describe the day to a partner.

Start up

1 Discuss the questions with a partner.

1 Which do you think is more common – a job for life or many different jobs?
2 Which would you prefer to have and why?
3 Can you get promoted more quickly by staying with one company or by moving companies?

Vocabulary

2 Read the text about careers. Then complete the sentences 1–7 with a highlighted word from the text.

In the past in the UK, many people had a career for life, that is until they decided to retire. There was often a very clear career path, so people knew where they would be in a certain number of years. A key part of this was the appraisal, where your manager would assess your performance each year or every six months. A good appraisal could mean that you climbed the career ladder much faster by being promoted quickly. Appraisals are still important, but they're just as important for a good reference as they are for getting promoted. Many people, when they don't get promoted as fast as they hoped, choose to resign and look for another job. Of course, it works the other way as well. You wouldn't be fired (or sacked) for a bad appraisal, unless you had done something wrong, but the company could choose not to promote you. In bad economic times, people's job insecurity often increases, so a good appraisal can make people feel more secure.

1 He was .... for stealing from the company.
2 He's only twenty, but he's already got his .... mapped out until he's 50, which is when he wants to ....
3 He has been .... faster than any other manager. He's really climbing the .... quickly.
4 My .... went really well. My boss said I was performing exceptionally. I didn't tell him I had applied for a new job, but at least it means I will get a good ....
5 So you got the new job. When are you going to .... ?
6 .... is one of the biggest causes of dissatisfaction in this company.
7 We have three-monthly reviews to .... our progress.

3 Discuss the questions with a partner.

1 Do you have appraisals at work?
2 When was your last appraisal?
3 What kind of questions are asked during your appraisals?

Say it right

4 Which syllable is stressed in each word? Write the words from the box in the correct column.

appraisal	assess	career	fire	ladder	promote	resign	retire

Oo	oO	oOo

5)) 2.2 Listen and check.

More practice

Listening

6 Look at the questions. Which ones are about past and current experiences and which are about future objectives?

1 Has the past year been good/bad/satisfactory for you, and why?
2 What do you consider to be your most important achievements of the past year?
3 What do you like and dislike about working for this organisation?
4 What elements of your job do you find most difficult?
5 What do you consider to be your most important aims and tasks in the next year?
6 What kind of work or job would you like to be doing in three years' time?

7 ⋙ 2.3 Listen to Gareth having his appraisal with his manager and make notes about each question in **6**.

8 ⋙ 2.4 Match the two parts to make phrases used to provide feedback. Listen to check your answers.

1 Overall, we think your work	a with the way you …
2 Your contribution here	b means that we …
3 You're doing really well,	c strengths is …
4 I'm particularly pleased	d job there …
5 One of your key	e so keep it up …
6 You've done a good	f is excellent.

9 Appraisal forms are often filled out before the interview. Imagine you have an appraisal for a job you are very dissatisfied with. Answer the questions in **6**.

10 Work with a partner and role play an appraisal. Remember to ask questions and provide feedback.

Vocabulary

11 Appraisals can often ask you to evaluate your skills in a particular area of work. Match the words in the box with the areas of work.

More practice

accessibility accuracy decisiveness delegating education empathy fairness goal setting honesty initiative innovation knowledge base listening loyalty originality prioritising productivity reliability teamwork training

Quality and quantity of work	
Communication and interpersonal skills	
Planning and organisation	
Leadership	
Job knowledge and expertise	
Attitude	
Ethics	
Creative thinking	

12 How would you rate yourself using the following scale on each of the areas in **11**?

1–3 = poor, 4–6 = satisfactory, 7–9 = good, 10 = excellent

Speaking

13 Discuss your rating with a partner. Complete the sentences with ideas for how you plan to improve your weaknesses.

I'm going to …   I intend to …   I need to think about …

1 Read the company profile and underline changes Arco, an online bookstore, has made in the last year.

COMPANY PROFILE

Arco is an online book retailer with warehouses across six European countries. It employs 2,000 people in total and last year took on an additional 200 people. The company has created between 200 and 500 new jobs every year for the last five years. Arco has promoted many of its original employees, but last year it hired many new external people for senior positions. Employees were getting large bonuses every year until last year, when the company decided to spend all the profits on entering two new markets. Salaries increased by 3% last year, but senior management salaries increased by 30%. Many of the company's first employees were quite young and last year an increasing number were taking time off for maternity leave and paternity leave. The company had a flexible working policy, but because so many people were asking for increasingly flexible hours, they stopped all flexitime. Employees had a lot of autonomy in the past, but last year more responsibility and control was given to managers and a stronger hierarchy was created.

2 Work in pairs. Read the staff satisfaction questionnaire sent to employees of Arco. Discuss which questions you think will have positive answers and which ones will have negative answers.

	1: very dissatisfied	2: dissatisfied	3: satisfied	4: very satisfied
1 To what extent are you satisfied with your promotion prospects?				
2 Are you happy with your career path so far?				
3 Are you satisfied with your salary?				
4 Are you satisfied with other working conditions? e.g. holiday, pension, bonuses				
5 Are you satisfied with your work-life balance?				
6 Are you satisfied with how your line manager manages your work?				

3))) 2.5 Listen to two managers from Arco discussing the results of the staff survey. Tick (✓) the relevant boxes in the survey in 2.

4 Work in groups of three. Student A, read the file on page 96. Student B, read the file on page 100. Student C, read the file on page 101. Make notes in your section of the table about the main problems.

Career path and promotion	Salary and conditions	Management and work-life balance

5 Ask and answer questions in your groups to complete the rest of the table.

6 Discuss the changes they could make in your group. Try to put them in order of importance.

7 Read the company memo to find out what changes were made. Which ones were similar to and which were different from your suggestions?

Dear employees,

In response to the staff survey, we will be making several changes this year and next. Bonuses from now on will be directly linked to profits. This will give you a better idea of how much to expect so that you can plan your personal finances. We will also put in place clear rules for promotion. We have grown very quickly in recent years, but our systems haven't grown with them. It will now be easier for you to see what else you need to do to get promoted. Next week, we will also be having staff sessions on work-life balance to help both you and us to develop a better understanding of how to manage the two.

We look forward to continuing to work with such a valuable team over the coming year.

Regards
Arco Management

Decision making
How do you decide?

Start up

1 How decisive are you? Circle the number that best matches your answer.

	often	sometimes	rarely	never
1 Do you have second thoughts after making a decision?	1	2	3	4
2 Do the opinions of others influence your decisions more than necessary?	1	2	3	4
3 Do you worry for a long time about difficult decisions?	1	2	3	4
4 Do you think about so many details that it is hard to make a decision?	1	2	3	4
5 Do you delay making decisions more than necessary?	1	2	3	4
6 Do you put too much energy into small decisions?	1	2	3	4
7 Do you let others take decisions for you that are really your decisions to make?	1	2	3	4
8 Have you missed opportunities because you waited too long to decide?	1	2	3	4
9 Did you hesitate as you answered these questions?	1	2	3	4

CHECK YOUR SCORE:

28–36:   You are very decisive and are happy with the way things are working in your life.

20–27:   You don't like making decisions. Sometimes you are great at it, but sometimes you can't decide what to do. Try to be decisive more often.

Below 20: You need to be more decisive. You probably have a major decision to make right now. You hope it will go away or that someone will make it for you.

2 Discuss your responses with a partner.

Reading

3 Read the texts and match the statements 1–4 with the types of decision maker.

1 'Why didn't you tell me that before? I really don't like finding things out so late!'

2 'Look, make your mind up, will you?! This is getting ridiculous.'

3 'I really wouldn't like to move forward on this unless everyone is happy.'

4 'We're not planning it all out today. Let's just think about the bigger picture.'

TYPES OF DECISION MAKERS

Controlling types are those who want all the information in a clear, focused and objective manner when someone puts forward an idea. They hate indecision and don't like to delay a decision. These people want to know what the benefits are, how soon it can be done, and what the bottom line is. If people don't do these things, they can be bossy, or aggressive.

Creative types are entrepreneurial. They value creativity and energy and are likely to trust their instincts. When they listen to other people's ideas, they immediately imagine how it will help them achieve their goals. Creative types find talking about detail, routine and processes boring, so they will become impatient or stop listening if you discuss these.

Peacemakers value close working relationships. They want to know that you're dependable and that what you're recommending will be beneficial for all concerned. They can easily be pushed into making a decision they don't agree with because they want to avoid confrontation and then later become difficult to work with. Peacemakers like to know all the details so that they can weigh up the options and minimise the risk. Ultimately, because relationships are so important, they want to reach a consensus.

Analysts think that they can't make their mind up until they know everything. Being correct, accurate, precise and logical in any proposal or decision is highly important. If they have to decide between two things, they need all the information so that they can justify their decision logically. Analytical decision makers hate surprises and unpredictability.

4 Discuss with a partner which type of decision maker you think you are.

Vocabulary

5 Match the verbs 1–8 with the phrases a–h to make verb phrases from ③.

1	put forward	a	a consensus
2	reach	b	my instincts
3	avoid	c	confrontation
4	make up	d	your mind
5	weigh up	e	between (two things)
6	trust	f	an idea / ideas
7	decide	g	a decision
8	delay	h	all the options

6 Complete the sentences with phrases from ⑤.

1 I really don't like arguments, so I'm always trying to ....

2 It's not a difficult decision. Can you just ....?

3 I can't .... the salmon or the sea bass.

4 I think we need to .... until next week.

5 I .... so many .... , but my boss just never listens to me.

6 We finally managed to .... I can't believe it took so long to get everyone to agree.

7 This isn't an easy decision. We need to .... very carefully.

8 I'm sorry, but I'm going to .... I just don't think we should go with the idea.

More practice

Say it right

7 ◄))) 3.1 Listen to how the underlined sound is pronounced in each word.

make, avoid, weigh, decide, delay

8 Circle the correct word in each case.

/eɪ/	display	enjoy	high
/ɔɪ/	choice	outline	remain
/aɪ/	review	provide	option

9 ◄))) 3.2 Listen and check your answers.

10 ◄))) 3.3 Listen and practise saying the sentences.

1 I find it difficult to make decisions.
2 Why do you always avoid making decisions?
3 Did you weigh up the options carefully?
4 When do we have to decide by?
5 I don't think we should delay the decision any further.

Speaking

11 Work with a partner and discuss the questions.

1 Is it important for you to reach a consensus?
2 Do you try to avoid confrontation?
3 Do you find it frustrating when people can't make their mind up?
4 Do you trust your instincts when making decisions?

Start up

1 Work with a partner and discuss the questions.

1 What staff training does your company provide?
2 What do you think makes a good training session?
3 Do you ever go on training days or to conferences? If so, tell your partner about it.

2 What do you think you would have to plan and arrange to organise a conference?

Reading

3 Read the text about the International CES and answer the questions.

1 Who's Jack Wayman?
2 When did the International CES start?
3 How has the International CES changed over the past 40 years?

The biggest conference in the world

From being a salesman in a shop, Jack Wayman went on to start what has become probably the largest trade show in the world, the International CES. The event has launched some of the most famous electronics products in history; from the Camcorder and Compact Disc Player in 1981 to Tablets, Netbooks and Android Devices in recent years. But its start in 1967, which attracted some 200 exhibitors and 17,500 delegates, faced many challenges. The planned venue, McCormick Place in Chicago, burned down right in front of Jack's eyes in January and the exhibition had to be quickly moved to a new location in New York City!

When the International CES started, it was all very different. A simple one-paragraph contract with all suppliers from caterers and hospitality through to photography was all that was needed. Today the show has expanded to include a programme of 500 speakers giving a range of talks, workshops with more audience involvement and demonstrations of products. CEOs rank it as one of their top 10 most desired speaking opportunities. Not surprising when there are 3,000 exhibitors, 5,000 journalists and analysts and nearly 150,000 delegates from over 140 countries.

4 Complete the sentences with a highlighted word from the text in **3**.

1 A conference is a professional development .... where people go to learn, network and present.
2 .... mainly involve listening to a speaker, whereas .... involve more audience interaction.
3 At a trade show, companies give many .... of their products to try to get orders.
4 .... often have a stand to attract customers and get interest in their products or services.
5 Some .... attend as .... at a conference, but most people attend to listen to others present.
6 The size of the .... can impact on the type of conference it will attract.
7 The .... tells everyone what's on when and where.
8 .... are responsible for all sorts of services such as food and drink and often outside .... are hired to prepare the food.

Listening

5 ◍))) **3.4** Listen to Sanjay and Meiko at a conference together. Complete the table with the information in the box.

food   presenters   venue   location

	Venue	Positives	Negatives
This year	Athens		
Last year	Vancouver		
Two years ago	Brighton		

6 Listen again and complete the sentences.

1 The food was certainly .... last year. I think this is probably the .... food I've ever had at a conference.
2 That really was the .... food ever. The presenters were at least .... in Brighton.
3 The venue is much .... and .... than here.
4 At least Athens is .... to get to than Brighton.
5 I think this is the .... it's ever been.
6 Last year was probably .... , it's just the Vancouver venue was bigger than here.

Grammar

Comparatives and superlatives

1 One-syllable adjectives: add *-er* or *-est* after the last consonant.

cheap   cheaper   the cheapest

2 For a short adjective ending in a vowel and consonant, double the final consonant.

big   bigger   the biggest

3 Two-syllable adjectives ending in -*y*: change the *y* to *i* and add *-er* or *-est*.

busy   busier   the busiest

4 Two or more syllables not ending in -*y*: put *more* or *the most* before the adjective.

interesting   more interesting   the most interesting

》》》GRAMMAR REFERENCE PAGE 105

More practice

7 Which rule is being used in each sentence in **6**? Which adjectives are irregular?

8 Complete the paragraph with the correct comparative or superlative form of the adjective in brackets.

Business tourism is one of the *most lucrative* ....¹ (lucrative) sectors of tourism. In the UK, it's one quarter of all tourism and is worth £16 billion. However, many other countries are *better* ....² (good) than the UK at getting delegates to stay on for a holiday. Conference visitors to France spend on average 4.5 days there, one day *longer* ....³ (long) than delegates to UK conferences. This extra day is worth £50 million and could create 1,700 jobs, so how do you make a country *more* ....⁴ (attractive)? Giving information at the *earliest* ....⁵ (early) possibility is important as it allows people to plan and organise their trip. The *most* ....⁶ (successful) events sell the conference and the city. Working with the local tourist office and the *best* ....⁷ (good) attractions to offer *cheapest* ....⁸ (cheap) entrance to delegates can help. Conference organisers can get *highest* ....⁹ (high) attendance figures by selling the city and not just the conference.

Speaking

9 Discuss the questions with a partner.

• Have you ever stayed on for a holiday after a conference?
• How could conference organisers persuade delegates to stay on for a holiday in your country?
• How could the last training day or conference you went on have been better?

Start up

1 Read the statements and decide how you would feel in each situation.

1 Somebody keeps interrupting you and talking over you.
2 People are not listening to your opinion at work.
3 Someone you work with keeps disagreeing with every idea you have.
4 Someone gives their opinions very directly and doesn't worry about people's feelings.

2 Share your opinions with a partner.

Reading

3 Read the text and match the headings with sections a–c.

1 Dealing with conflict   2 Going forward   3 Avoiding conflict

Conflict with family, friends and co-workers can cause a lot of stress, but it can be avoided by following a few simple tips.

a ____

Expressing disagreement is an essential way of sharing our opinions and understanding other people's ideas, but we don't need to go to war in every argument.

- **Watch your triggers.** Write down all the subjects that get you 'hot under the collar'. If you know what makes you angry, you can control yourself better when they come up in conversation.
- **Be selective.** You don't have to express disagreement every time. Think 'Is it worth it?' before you start to argue.
- **Leave before things get bad.** Step back if you think you're going to shout. When you're calmer you can express your feelings better and people will listen to you more.

b ____

Sometimes it's impossible to avoid conflict and we have to argue. This is fine, but it's very important to manage the argument so it doesn't get out of control. Here's some advice.

- **Don't forget to listen.** Listening to what other people have to say is very important. It helps you understand why they think that way, so you can choose the best reply.
- **Agree on something.** Try and find at least one thing that you agree on and then say that you agree. After that, people will listen to your opinions more.
- **Don't get personal.** It's very important to stay focused on the subject of the argument. Don't start arguing about you or the other person.
- **Find a win-win situation.** There doesn't have to be a loser in all conflicts, so you don't have to beat your opponent. Try and find a solution where both sides are winners.
- **Admit when you're wrong.** Keep an open mind and listen to all the opinions. If you realise you're wrong about something, admit it and move on.

c ____

After an argument there are many opportunities to make friendships and professional relationships even stronger.

- **Don't forget to say thank you.** When an argument is over, express appreciation at how the other person helped to resolve it. You can even remind them of good points that they made.
- **Move forward.** After the disagreement, the best thing to do is change the subject and talk about something else. Why not go for a coffee and find out something new about the other person?

4 Match each person with a piece of advice they should follow from the text.

1 I find I get angrier and angrier, and don't know when to stop.
2 I often don't hear what the other person has to say – I'm just thinking about my view.
3 Whenever he mentions the Milton project, it makes me mad.
4 I find other people are wrong much more often than I am.
5 I always end up arguing about what the other person did years ago.
6 Sometimes, the most important thing for me is winning the argument.
7 I can't speak to someone for ages after an argument.

Listening

5 3.5 Mona, Ahmed and Chintel are in a meeting. They are choosing hotels to recommend to delegates coming to a conference. Which of the hotels do they decide on?

HOTEL

City Travel | Myatt | Madison | Flight Link | Berkeley | Parkside

6 Listen again and match the hotels with the comments.

1 Myatt	a has a spa and a good location.
2 Madison	b is $10 more expensive than Flight Link.
3 City Travel	c has a spa and fantastic food.
4 Flight Link	d is nice, but expensive.
5 Parkside	e is 20% cheaper than the Myatt.
6 Berkeley	f is terrible.

7 Work with a partner and complete the phrases from the meeting.

1 From my p_ _sp_ct_ _ _ …
2 I agree with you up to a p_ _n_.
3 I couldn't _g_ _ _ more.
4 Yes, b_t …
5 I'm not s_ _e about that.
6 As far as I'm c_ _c_ _n_d …
7 That's f_ _ _ with me.
8 The d_ _w_a_k is …

8 Listen to the meeting extract again and check your answers.

9 Write the phrases from **7** in the correct column.

1 Giving your opinion	2 Agreeing	3 Disagreeing	4 Partly agreeing/disagreeing

Speaking

10 What decisions do you regularly have to make at work? Try to think of eight different decisions and put them on the chart below.

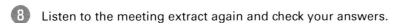

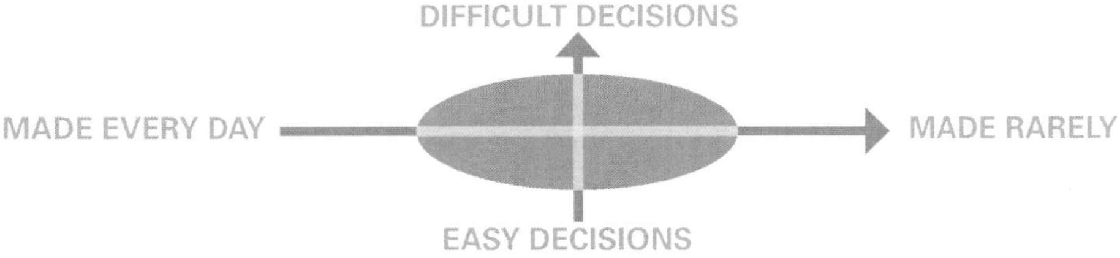
DIFFICULT DECISIONS
MADE EVERY DAY
MADE RARELY
EASY DECISIONS

11 Work with a partner. Choose two or three decisions from your chart and explain the options involved.

12 Take one decision from each of your lists and role play a meeting using phrases from this lesson.

Student A	Student B
Give your opinion on the decision. Give a reason to support your opinion.	Disagree with your partner's decision. Agree with your partner to a certain extent.

Scenario: The best option

1 Look at the pictures and match them with the words in the box.

> buffet   canapés   carvery   sit-down meal

2 Red Lantern Publishing is launching a major new book soon and wants to organise a launch event. With a partner, try to think of an advantage and a disadvantage for each of the dining options in **1**.

3))) **3.6** Listen to Miguel and Karen discussing the event and complete the notes.

4 Work in groups of three. Student A, read the text on page 27. Student B, read the text on page 96. Student C, read the text on page 101. Make notes in your section of the table below.

> Number of guests: 200 [1]
> Total budget: £ 8,000 [2]
> Food and drinks budget depends on
> the venue [3]. Minimum £ 20 – [4] per
> head. Maximum £ 40 [5] per head.
> Venue – option 1 a bookshop [6] – option 2
> the castle [7] – option 3 The Bands [8]
> Rochester

	Student A	Student B	Student C
Venue			
Location			
Cost			
Food option 1			
Food option 1 cost			
Food option 2			
Food option 2 cost			

Student A

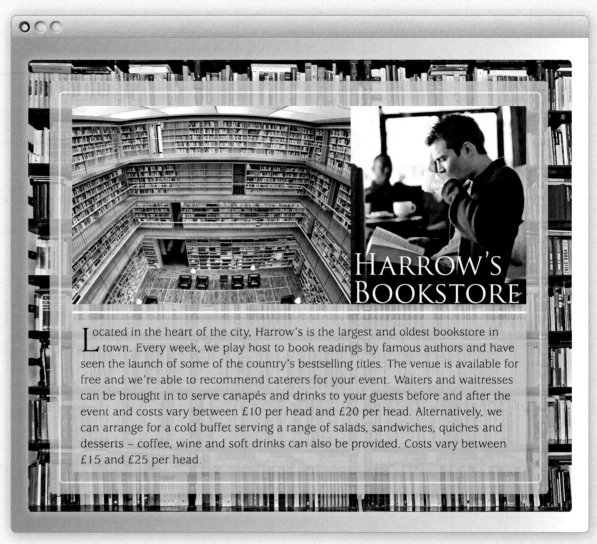

HARROW'S BOOKSTORE

Located in the heart of the city, Harrow's is the largest and oldest bookstore in town. Every week, we play host to book readings by famous authors and have seen the launch of some of the country's bestselling titles. The venue is available for free and we're able to recommend caterers for your event. Waiters and waitresses can be brought in to serve canapés and drinks to your guests before and after the event and costs vary between £10 per head and £20 per head. Alternatively, we can arrange for a cold buffet serving a range of salads, sandwiches, quiches and desserts – coffee, wine and soft drinks can also be provided. Costs vary between £15 and £25 per head.

5 Report back to your group on what you think are the advantages and disadvantages of your location.

6 Discuss the questions in your group.
1 Which venue would be easiest for guests to get to?
2 Which venue would create the best impression?
3 Which food option is best for each venue?

7 Student A, look below. Student B, look at page 96. Student C, look at page 101.

Student A
You're very keen on the bookstore and the canapé option. It would only cost £4,000 so you could spend money on other things for the guests. You would like to book live music and give all the guests a gift bag when they leave. You think the atmosphere is more important than the food and want to give people a night to remember.

8 Role play your meeting to make your decision.

4 Careers
Working conditions

Start up

1 Put these factors in order of importance and compare your results with a partner.

a good salary		helping people	
prestige or status		responsibility and power	
holidays and time off		the opportunity to be creative	
flexible working conditions		short hours	

2 Which of the factors from **1** do you think are connected to each of these jobs?

> footballer   hotel manager   lawyer   nurse

Reading

3 Investment bankers are often paid very well, but have to work long hours.
Tell a partner whether you think the job is worth such a high salary. Why/Why not?

4 Polly Courtney worked for an investment bank before becoming an author.
Read the text. Why did she want the job with the bank and why did she leave it?

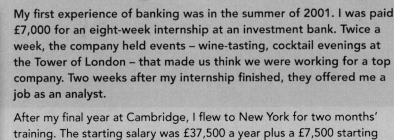

Worth the money?

Golden Handcuffs
The lowly life of a high flyer

"For everyone who has been, wants to be or is already there"

Polly Courtney

My first experience of banking was in the summer of 2001. I was paid £7,000 for an eight-week internship at an investment bank. Twice a week, the company held events – wine-tasting, cocktail evenings at the Tower of London – that made us think we were working for a top company. Two weeks after my internship finished, they offered me a job as an analyst.

After my final year at Cambridge, I flew to New York for two months' training. The starting salary was £37,500 a year plus a £7,500 starting bonus, at a time when average graduate salaries were around £20,000. We were 300 ambitious youngsters in Manhattan with a lot of money. It was the most exciting but exhausting summer of my life.

However, the hours were much longer than during the internship. I was one of the lucky ones. I often left work before midnight, and rarely spent a full weekend in the office. Other first-years weren't so lucky. One guy was sent home suffering from exhaustion after working all night for two days.

It wasn't so much the number of working hours but the fact that they were always changing. Occasionally, I arranged to meet a friend at 9.00 p.m. However, at 6.30 p.m, a director would give me more work, saying 'Could you just ...' and finishing with 'and if you could have that on my desk by seven o'clock tomorrow morning, that would be great'. There was enough work to fill eight hours!

One night I left at 11.00 p.m. and went home to bed. I was sleeping soundly, but my doorbell woke me at 1.00 a.m. They wanted me back in the office and had sent a taxi driver round to wake me up. They had tried calling my mobile, but I hadn't heard it. I went back to the office and worked nearly 24 hours.

Seeing my friends at Christmas finalised my decision to leave. They reminded me that there was more to life. Other people weren't so sure. There was the chance of a big pay rise and bonus for those who stayed. There's always something round the corner, making you want to stay. Of the 32 graduates who joined in my year, there are three left today and all have moved out of that department.

5 Read the text again and complete Polly's job description.

Job title	
Starting salary	
Working hours	
Benefits	

6 Would you like to do Polly's job? Are the advantages more important than the disadvantages?

Vocabulary

7 Write the words from the box in the correct column.

> bonus   commission   experience   flexitime   full-time   gym membership   hire
> make redundant   overtime   (paid) holiday   pay rise   sack   sick leave   skills
> subsidised canteen   take on   wages

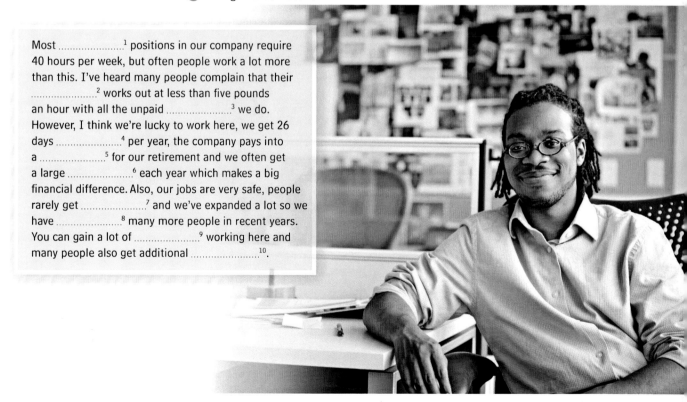
More practice

Money	Working hours	Benefits	Hiring and firing	Personal profile
salary	part-time	pension	employ	qualifications
pay			lay off	

8 Complete the text describing Ivan's job at a record company with some of the words from the table in **7** using the correct form.

Most ....[1] positions in our company require 40 hours per week, but often people work a lot more than this. I've heard many people complain that their ....[2] works out at less than five pounds an hour with all the unpaid ....[3] we do. However, I think we're lucky to work here, we get 26 days ....[4] per year, the company pays into a ....[5] for our retirement and we often get a large ....[6] each year which makes a big financial difference. Also, our jobs are very safe, people rarely get ....[7] and we've expanded a lot so we have ....[8] many more people in recent years. You can gain a lot of ....[9] working here and many people also get additional ....[10].

Writing

9 Write a description of your current job (or ideal job). Talk about the salary, working hours, benefits and your level of job satisfaction.

Start up

1 How do companies recruit new employees? Put the stages in the correct order.

...4... Shortlist the candidates
...2... Advertise the position
...1... Write the job description
...3... Read CVs and covering letters or application forms
...5... Invite successful candidates for an interview
...7... Offer the best candidate the job
...6... Set some selection tests

2 Which is the most difficult part of applying for a job for you? Compare your ideas with a partner.

Reading

3 Read Tiago Costa and Anna Luiz's applications for a post as sales director. What do the numbers refer to?

2007   2010   18   3   6   2008

Tiago Costa

I have a lot of sales experience and I have worked in three different sectors – insurance, property and the motor industry. I have been extremely successful in sales and have always developed good relationships with my customers. I studied Psychology at Newcastle University and I graduated in 2008. The first job I had was as a car salesman for an Audi dealership. After a year at Audi, I worked for an insurance company, selling home insurance. In October 2010, I joined a property company called Edward's and I won their Salesperson of the Year award after only six months at the company.

Anna Luiz

I have worked in the retail sector for several years and have really enjoyed my career. I left school in 2004, when I was 18, and I have worked for two different companies. My first job was as a sales assistant in a men's clothing store. After a year there, I was promoted to assistant manager. I left that company in 2007 and joined a supermarket chain as a store manager. My store made record profits in 2010, so all my staff received a large bonus as a thank you.

Grammar

More practice

Tense	Use	Form
Past simple	To talk about finished actions in the past. It is often used when we know the exact time of the action. **yesterday, last month, in 2005**	Most regular verbs add -ed. play – played Verbs ending in -e add -d only. dance – danced Verbs ending in -y drop the -y and add -ied. carry – carried Many verbs have an irregular past form become – became go – went
Present perfect	To talk about general experiences not at a precise time. **I've been to Madrid.** To describe the duration of things still true at the present time. **She's lived in Lisbon for five years.** We often use *for* and *since* with the present perfect.	I/We/They/You + *have* ('ve) He/She/It + *has* ('s) + the past participle of the verb I've been to Madrid. She's lived in Lisbon for five years. He's worked here since 2010.

››› GRAMMAR REFERENCE PAGE 106

4 <u>Underline</u> the verbs in the texts in **3**. Say which tense they are.

5 Complete the texts with the correct form of the present perfect or past simple.

Tiago

Interviewer: *Have you ever had* [1] (you ever / have) any management experience?

Tiago: I *have had* [2] (have) some, but not very much. I *managed* [3] (manage) two trainee members of staff last year. It was a good experience and I *learned* [4] (learn) a lot.

Interviewer: *Did you* [5] (you / have) any challenges to deal with?

Tiago: No, not really. I *have found* [6] (find) the position quite easy.

Interviewer: What *has been* [7] (be) the hardest challenge for you in your career so far?

Tiago: Some people find direct selling hard, but for me, customer service *has been* [8] (be) the most challenging. Before my last position, I *worked* [9] (work) in a customer-facing post and sometimes the customers *were* [10] (be) difficult to handle.

Anna

Interviewer: When you were a sales assistant, *did you reach* [11] (you / reach) your sales targets every month?

Anna: Yes, I *did* [12] (do) and after one year, the manager *promoted* [13] (promote) me to assistant manager.

Interviewer: Why *did you* [14] (you / leave) the position?

Anna: I *felt* [15] (feel) I *needed* [16] (need) a new challenge and, in 2007, I *joined* [17] (join) my current company where I *have been* [18] (be) store manager for four years.

Interviewer: What *has been* [19] (be) your biggest challenge since joining your firm?

Anna: In my old job I *was* [20] (be) only responsible for five people but because of the success of our branch, I *have had* [21] (have) to increase staffing to 50 people. I *haven't* [22] (never / manage) *managed* so many people before.

Say it right **6** Write the words in the correct column.

answered played	/ɪd/	/d/	/t/
checked posted	Consulted	answered	checked
consulted pushed	decided	played	shipped
decided shipped	posted	stayed	laughed
emailed stayed	wanted	emailed	pushed
laughed wanted			

7 ◁))) 4.1 Listen and check.

Listening **8** ◁))) 4.2 On the company's website, Anna and Tiago find someone talking about working for the company. Listen to the description. Student A, complete the table below. Student B, complete the table on page 97.

Student A	
When did he start work?	He started work in 2007
What was his first job?	His first job was as a junior sales manager
Which departments has he been responsible for?	He has been the manager of men's clothing, women's clothing and household goods

9 Write your answers in full sentences using the present perfect or past simple.

10 Show your partner your sentences but cover the questions. What does your partner think the questions were?

Speaking **11** Tell your partner about three specific events in your past working life and three general experiences.

I left school in 2006 and started work in a hotel.   *I've never managed people.*

Start up

1 Read the quotations about first impressions and discuss them with a partner. Which do you agree/disagree with?

'It only takes three to five seconds to make a first impression, but it can take a whole career to undo it.' *Dana May Casperson*

'I don't like that man. I must get to know him better.' *Abraham Lincoln*

'It's only at first encounter, that a face makes its full impression on us.' *Arthur Schopenhauer*

2 Put the sentences in order of importance for making a good first impression.

....1.. Be on time.
....2.. Be yourself.
....7.. Don't always be right.
....5.. Look smart.
....4.. Prepare for small talk.
....3.. Show good listening skills.
....6.. Use the other person's name.

Listening

3 ◁))) **4.3** Carolina's going on a sales conference to Milan. She meets a lot of new people and people she knows from the past. Listen to three short conversations. Number the sentences.

a Carolina's introducing herself and her company.   2
b Carolina's introducing two people. 1
c Carolina's greeting someone she knows. 3

4 Look at the expressions for meeting and greeting. Match the expressions 1–9 with the responses a–i.

1 Nice to see you again. c
2 Have you met Christiana? e
3 What does your company do? a
4 May I join you?
5 I'd like you to meet Maria. b
6 How's everything going? g
7 You must be Lucy. h
8 Where are you based? d
9 Where does your company operate? f

3 a We publish primary school books.
5 b Nice to meet you.
1 c Good to see you again, too.
8 d In Rio.
2 e No, I don't believe I have.
9 f We have branches across the whole of Latin America.
6 g Not too bad, thanks.
7 h That's right.
4 i Sure.

5 ·))) 4.4 Listen and check your answers. Which situation(s) from 3 could Carolina use each of these expressions in?

6 ·))) 4.5 Listen to four more conversations during Carolina's trip. What's the topic of each?
1 ..C....   a talking about the conference
2 ..a....   b talking about your journey
3 ..d....   c describing your job
4 ..B....   d talking about your hometown

Speaking

7 Imagine you are at a conference and you have to have similar conversations to those in 6. What would you say in response to each of these questions?
1 What do you do?
2 What do you think of it so far?
3 How was the flight?
4 What was the traffic like?
5 So is your hometown a historic town?

8 Work with a partner. Try to think of more questions you could ask for the topics in 6, then practise the following conversation:
• Introduce yourself.
• Discuss three of the things from 6.
• Introduce your partner to somebody else.

Scenario: The right person for the job

1 Match the positive personal qualities 1–8 with the negative opposites a–h.

1 well-organised *b*	a apathetic and demotivated
2 adaptable/flexible *f*	b badly-organised
3 honest *c*	c dishonest
4 friendly and outgoing *g*	d habitually late
5 enthusiastic and motivated *a*	e individualistic
6 punctual *d*	f inflexible
7 a good team-player *e*	g unfriendly/reserved
8 creative *h*	h unimaginative

2 Read the job advertisement. Which qualities from **1** would you need for the responsibilities listed in the advertisement.

○ ○ ○

Job description: Hotel Manager

You will be responsible for the day-to-day management of the hotel and its staff. The work will vary from day to day so a flexible approach is required.

Your typical responsibilities will include:

• budgeting and financial management
• planning, organising and directing all hotel services
• food and beverage operations
• housekeeping
• recruiting, training and monitoring staff
• planning the work schedules for individuals and teams.

Customer focused, you will be an expert in all areas of customer service, in particular dealing with complaints. The hotel has a number of conferences and wedding functions every month and you will need to ensure these run smoothly. While taking a strategic overview and planning ahead to maximise profits, the manager must also set an example for staff meeting guests' needs and expectations. Business and people management are equally important elements.

3 Work with a partner. Student A, look at the notes on page 35 for Theo and Darren. Student B, look at the notes for Susan and Jenny on page 97. Ask and answer questions to find out about each candidate's experience. Complete the table.

Essential experience	Theo	Darren	Susan	Jenny
Planning and organising	Yes	No	Yes	Yes
Managing teams	Yes	Yes	No	Yes
Customer service skills	No	Yes	Yes	Yes
Budgeting and financial skills	Yes	No	No	Yes
Desired experience	Yes	Yes	Yes	Yes
Work in a hotel or similar environment	No	Yes	Yes	Yes
Track record of delivering a profit			No	Yes
Recruiting and training staff			No	Yes
Foreign language skills	Yes		Yes	No

Student A

Name: Theo Charalambides
Education: Master's degree in Business Administration. Bachelor's degree in Accounting and Finance. Chartered Accountant.
Experience: He's worked for many large finance companies in London. He studied to become a chartered accountant and passed his exams in 2004. He hasn't got any customer service experience, but he has got a lot of strategic and financial experience. A key part of his role was the recruitment and training of staff. He left his job to look for new challenges.
Skills: Fluent in Greek, German and French.

Name: Darren Tasker
Education: Master's degree in English Literature:
Experience: He travelled for two years after leaving university. He worked in restaurants around the world as a waiter. When he returned to the UK, he got a job as a head waiter. He's had a lot of management experience including recruiting and training staff. He's learnt a lot about budgeting and finance in his current post as manager of a very profitable restaurant chain.
Skills: Good IT skills. Basic French.

4 Discuss with a partner which candidate you think is most suitable for the job, and why.

5 The team decide not to interview Theo. Discuss with a partner why you think they made this decision.

6 Look at page 99 to find out if you were right.

7 ◄)) 4.6 Listen to an extract from each interview. Match the person with a description of the impression they give.

Essential experience	Darren	Susan	Jenny
1 Very likable and personable. Easy to get along with. Motivational speaker.			✓
2 Very smart and professional appearance. Good first impression. A bit too self-confident, with a high level of self-belief.		✓	
3 Very driven, hard-working and ambitious, but cold and distant.	✓		

8 ◄)) 4.7 Listen to the interview panel discussing the three candidates. Make notes about the experience and interviewers' impressions of each candidate.

	Experience	Impression
Darren Tasker	stronger experience. ambitious	best candidates. cold and distant
Susan De Costa	successfull in business before not in the same sector.	love this person Proffessional confident and a bit arrogant.
Jenny Flynn	excellente manager - staff and costumers	Vary outsantanding excellent interview. Puts herself in the teams position

9 Based on this extra information you have of each, would you change your mind?

Soft capabilities

modal verbs for advice, obligation and necessity – *must* and *mustn't*, *have to* and *don't have to*, *should* and *shouldn't*

Start up

1 Look at the sentences about behaviour in different countries. Choose the country you think is correct.

1 *Americans/Argentinians* like to get straight to the point in meetings.
2 In *France/Korea*, many large businesses are family run.
3 In *Germany/the UK*, bosses are often subject specialists.
4 In *Brazil/Singapore*, showing emotions is a sign of enthusiasm, not a loss of control.
5 *Americans/Japanese people* frequently use humour in business situations.
6 Time is a very flexible concept in *Norway/Saudi Arabia*.

2 Discuss with a partner which statements in **1** are similar to and which are different from your country.

Reading

3 Lars Eklo is going to work in Argentina. Alain Bassong has worked there before. Read Alain's email providing some advice and complete the notes.

1 It's not unusual to have colleagues that are friends in .....Argentina.....
2 Using first names with peers is common in .....France.....
3 Plans are short term in .....Argentina.....
4 It isn't always clear who makes the decisions in .....Argentina.....
5 Late changes are often made to plans in .....Argentina.....

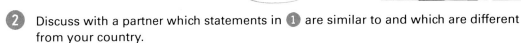

I work for a French company in Paris and recently spent quite a lot of time working with an Argentinian company. I can't speak Spanish and they can't speak French, so the language we had to use was English. Language wasn't the problem; it was understanding how each other worked.

Some things just happen a bit differently. I get on well with my colleagues, but they're not my best friends. For me, work is work and friends are friends! You don't have to socialise with colleagues in France, but in Argentina it's quite common. The managers have a much closer friendship with their subordinates, although in Argentina you should always use surnames. In France, you can use first names with peers, but not in Argentina.

One of the hardest things was our perspectives on time. In France, generally you should establish a long-term strategy, but you shouldn't expect this in Argentina. They were much more focused on the here and now and short-term plans. Also from our perspective, plans are quite fixed and we don't really change them without a lot of notice. It's really different in Argentina, as plans changed frequently at the last minute.

It was also very hard to work out who had the power to make decisions. Both countries have a strong hierarchy and you have to pay attention to status, but sometimes people you thought could make a decision couldn't or wouldn't, and it was made by others.

Meetings are quite similar – we're both passionate in our style; people speak at the same time and interrupt each other, but they also seem happy to disagree and even argue. In France, I would say that you mustn't disagree so strongly.

They probably found us a bit strange as well, but we're working together well now.

4 What advice is given in the text on how you address someone in Argentina?

Grammar

Modal verbs for advice

We use **should** and **shouldn't** to give and ask for advice.

You shouldn't focus on the long term in Argentina.

Should I dress smartly for meetings?

We use **must** and **mustn't** to give strong advice.

You must be flexible doing business in Argentina.

You mustn't strongly disagree in formal meetings.

》》》GRAMMAR REFERENCE PAGE 107

Listening

5 ·))) 5.1 Listen to Alain giving Lars advice on doing business in Argentina. Which of these does he give advice on?

1 meeting face-to-face
2 punctuality
3 conversations at the start of a meeting
4 being a manager
5 talking about work over dinner

More practice

6 Write sentences using *should, shouldn't, must* and *mustn't* to give advice on doing business in Argentina.

7 ·))) 5.2 What does Alain tell Lars about each of these things in Argentina?

1 visa
2 health care
3 money
4 travel

Grammar

Modal verbs – obligation and necessity

We use **must** when the obligation comes from the speaker.

Health care is very good, but you must get good insurance as it can be expensive.

We use **have to** when the obligation comes from someone else, e.g. a law.

Mustn't and **don't have to** are very different. **Don't have to** means it is not necessary, but **mustn't** means it is forbidden or not allowed.

You don't have to have one to travel there, but you have to get a visa to work there.

》》》GRAMMAR REFERENCE PAGE 107

8 Try to remember the conversation in **7** to complete the sentences about Argentina with the correct modal verb.

More practice

1 You .... have a visa to work there.
2 You .... get good health insurance.
3 You .... take a lot of money as it's cheaper than Paris.
4 You .... forget your passport when you use your credit card.

9 Listen again and check.

Speaking

10 Think about your own country. What advice would you give to someone coming to do business in your country? Work with a partner to produce a small cultural guide.

Start up   **1**   Look at the ten most popular tourist destinations in the world and tell a partner what you know about each city.

Paris | London | New York | Istanbul | Singapore | Kuala Lumpur | Hong Kong | Dubai | Bangkok | Antalya

Vocabulary   **2**   Complete the sentences about the ten cities using the words in the box.

> architecture   art gallery   beach   financial district   metropolitan area
> museum   park   shopping malls   skyscrapers   subway

More practice

1   New York City's .... is home to the New York Stock Exchange.
2   There are over 1,200 .... in Hong Kong, but Dubai has the tallest one – the Burj Khalifa.
3   Antalya is popular for its .... on the Mediterranean Sea.
4   The City of London only has about 10,000 inhabitants, but the .... has a population of just over twelve million. To get around, you can travel on the oldest .... in the world.
5   Istanbul has .... from around the world including temples, churches and mosques.
6   The Louvre .... is the most visited in the world with 8.5 million visitors per year.
7   Singapore's range of .... mean you can buy just about anything there.
8   A great place to see the rich cultural history of Malaysia is the National .... in Kuala Lumpur.
9   Lumpini .... in Bangkok is a large space with lakes, open air concerts and even a library.

3   Use the words from **2** to talk about what tourist attractions people can see in your city.

Reading   **4**   Read the text and find what the numbers refer to.

> 621,000   2.82 million   2014   40%   2016   378,000

Rio

Rio de Janeiro hosts the World Cup in 2014 and the Olympics in 2016 and is likely to be one of the most visited cities in the world. But Rio hasn't always had it so good.

Between 1985 and 1993, international airport arrivals fell from 621,000 to 378,000 per year and average hotel occupancy fell to 50%. There were poor services for tourists and many workers only spoke Portuguese. The beach and city were polluted and increasing crime against tourists made the city dangerous. Since then, the government has modernised the economy and improved the tourism industry. In 2008, 2.82 million international tourists came to Rio. So what can you see and do in Rio?

Perhaps one of the most famous images of Rio is the Christ Statue on Corcovado, and along with the Sugarloaf Mountain, it has some of the most spectacular views of Rio. The best way to reach the top of the Sugarloaf Mountain is the cable car, made famous by a fight scene in a James Bond film.

Nearly 40 per cent of all international travellers in Rio are on business with limited time. One of the best places to be when time is limited is Ipanema with its stunning beach, shops, cultural centres, and museums, all in walking distance. When the sun sets, the fun doesn't end. With a mix of cafés, bars and clubs serving chilled drinks and delicious food, there's always something happening. Stroll around Praça da Paz, Baixo Farme and Baixo Quitéria, watch live music, or sip fresh coconut under the stars at a beach kiosk. There's something for everyone here and you can see why the Brazilian hosts are so sociable and outgoing.

5 Read again and answer the questions.

1 What were the problems with Rio between 1985 and 1993? Find the problem each of the adjectives describes:

> dangerous   polluted   poor

2 Two things were done to improve the city: .... and ....
3 There are two places to get the best views of the city: from .... and ....
4 *Stroll* and *sip* mean .... and .... more slowly than normal. What's the writer trying to show about Rio?

6 Write the adjectives from the box in the correct column. Some words can go in more than one column.

lleno (lugar lleno de gente?)

antiguo → ancient   boring   busy   cosmopolitan   crowded   expensive   fast   fresh   frozen   modern   outgoing   plain   quiet   rude   shy   sociable   traditional

extrovertido   *→ maleducado*

Food	City	People
Fresh	Cosmopolitan	busy
frozen	modern	boring
traditional	Busy	shy
expensive	quiet	sociable
fast	Ancient	rude
Plain	Crowded	outgoing
modern	expensive	modern
	Quiet	Quiet

Listening

7))) 5.3 Listen and complete the sentences with words from **6**.

1
A: We don't have much time. Why don't we go to a café for some f..ast.... food?
B: That sounds like a good idea, and it's not e.xpensive.

2
A: It's so c.rowded. in here.
B: How about finding another bar? I know a nice q.uiet.... bar just round the corner.

3
A: I'm only in the city for one day. What should I do?
B: If I were you, I'd go to the market in the morning – it's really lively and b.usy......... You can buy f.resh...... snacks. Then go to the beach. Don't be s.hy........ – everyone's very s.ociable. and o.utgoing.

dinámico

4
A: That was the worst restaurant I've ever been to. R.ude........ staff, p.lain...... food and expensive.
B: They often are in Tourist areas. Perhaps we should go somewhere more t.raditional I really want to try the Feijoada. We might be better off booking though.

Speaking

8 Work with a partner. Student A, look below. Student B, look at the information on page 100.

You are a tourist in your partner's city. Ask for recommendations on:
• cheap restaurants • modern art galleries to visit • historic architecture.

Start up

1 **Look at the pictures and discuss the questions with a partner.**

1 Which pictures show something you're afraid of?

2 Do you have any other fears?

3 Why do you think people are afraid of public speaking?

4 What do you do to stay calm when you have to speak in public?

Reading

2 **Read the text and discuss the questions with a partner.**

1 Do you know of such events in your own country?

2 Do you know anyone that has their own business? If so, tell your partner about it.

3 What are the opportunities for people presenting their business ideas at these types of events?

Entrepreneurship

Small businesses are big business. Global Entrepreneurship Week was launched in 2008 by former UK Prime Minister Gordon Brown and Carl Schramm, the President and CEO of the Ewing Marion Kauffman Foundation. Since then, over seven million people from 115 countries have attended more than 37,000 activities held by nearly 24,000 partner organisations.

Brazil has fully embraced these entrepreneurial activities, with millions of people attending hundreds of events hosted by the Endeavour Brazil organisation.

Speakers and delegates have the opportunity to network, listen to business leaders and meet successful entrepreneurs such as Leila Velez, president of Brazilian beauty chain Beleza Natural, who spoke at the Dell Women's Entrepreneur Network event.

Leila and her partners developed a unique business that identified a real market need in Brazil: how to handle unruly, curly hair by enhancing it, not straightening it. The company now has 26 salons in Rio de Janeiro and São Paulo, which serve up to 1,000 customers a day. These events provide an opportunity to network and learn, as well as giving people the chance to present and gain potential investment in their own business idea.

Listening

3 Put the following in order of importance for delivering a good presentation.

delivery (voice) ☐   knowledge ☐
body language ☐   appearance ☐
technology ☐

4 ◀))) 5.4 Listen to a presentations expert talking about each of the features in **3**.
Complete the sentences on what makes a good presentation.

1 Think about your _audience's_ knowledge.
2 The content needs to be _Organized_ logically.
3 As a guideline, slides should have _six_ bullet points with _six_ words per line.
4 Be prepared for _technology_ to go wrong.
5 Good delivery means using _pauses_, stress and _intonation_ to maintain the audience's interest.
6 People won't understand if you speak _quickly_ and won't _pay attention_ if you speak too slowly.
7 _Eye_ contact and gestures can keep the audience's attention.
8 You should have a smart and professional _appearance_

5 ◀))) 5.5 Listen to an extract from a presentation. What's the main problem with the presentation?

6 ◀))) 5.6 Listen to the same presentation again. Try to notice where the speaker uses these features of a good presentation.

✓ pauses   ✓ rhetorical questions
✓ repetition   grouping of points in threes

7 Check your answers against the audioscript on page 122.

8 Write the phrases for structuring a presentation in the correct place in the table.

> As I said earlier …   First, I'm going to …   I have divided my presentation into ….
> I'd now like to turn my attention to …   If you remember, I mentioned before …   In conclusion …
> Let's get started   Moving on …   To elaborate on this …   To expand on this idea ….

Starting a presentation	Outlining a presentation	Expanding a point
• *Let me introduce myself* • Let's get started	• First, I'm going to • I have divide my presentation into	• To expand on this idea • To elaborate on
Repeating a point	**Changing to a new point**	**Concluding**
• As I said earlier • If you remember, I mentioned before	- Moving on • I'd now like to turn my attention to	*To sum up …* - In conclusion

Speaking

9 Choose a topic to give a presentation on.

• a business idea   • your job
• your company   • what motivates you

10 Prepare a presentation that will last 3–5 minutes.
Think about the structure and practise your delivery.

11 Deliver the presentation to the class.

Scenario: A job abroad

1 Imagine you're going to live and work in another country for six months. Discuss with a partner which of the things below would be most important to know. Can you add any more to the list?

- 1 · the best/worst places to live in the city
- 5 · local laws and customs
- 7 · local food
- 6 · where to buy things from your own country
- 2 · where to book lessons in the local language
- 3 · what the weather will be like

- 8 · are there many people from your own country?
- 4 · the rules/etiquette for working in the country
- 9 · things to bring from home
- 10 · local history
- 11 · local places of interest
- · other ....

2))) 5.7 Karim is in charge of managing new recruits to the Dubai office of Telecom DB. Listen to the voicemail and complete the notes.

> New group of employees coming to Dubai for ......6...... months from
> The UK.
> Need to find someone to give a presentation about ...living and working in Dubai

3 Karim asks Nick to find people who could give the presentation. Read Nick's email and the web links below and on page 43. Discuss with a partner which person you think would be better and why.

Hi Karim,

I've found three possible options for the presentation:

Mohammed Al-Amri is an employee here at Telecom DB. He was born in the UAE and has lived in Dubai for ten years, since he started with us. Being local, he obviously knows the customs well. He's got a family and will know about schools and things for people coming with their family. He's happy to give a presentation if we give him some guidance on what topics to cover.

Alternatively, we could look outside the company:

Chris Brown runs the British Society here in Dubai. It helps British people to settle here, find schools, join clubs and it runs a number of events every year. See their website below.

Ruben Limbu runs an intercultural training company helping people adjust to living and working in a different country. There's a link to their site below.

Best wishes

Nick

Are you new to Dubai
or moving here soon?

If so, then we can help you to settle here quickly. We've been running the society for fifteen years now and can provide advice on a number of issues such as the best places to live, where to find British shops and restaurants, which schools provide a British education and where to find the things that remind you of home. We run lots of lively events and have a British football league.

For any information, email us at britishsocietydubai@ymail.org or come along to one of our evenings at Morgan's Café.

○○○

ICT INTERCULTURAL TRAINING

Speaking a common language such as English does not always mean communication will be effective. It's also important to know about the different behaviour, attitudes and values of people from different cultures.

ICT has been working successfully in the field of intercultural training and consulting since 2000. Effective intercultural training can sometimes make the difference between success and failure in an international project. One part of our training is aimed at people relocating to other countries. The goal is to help them know and understand more about the country and culture they're moving to. Other training is intended for groups working in international teams or for those working with clients and colleagues from other countries. ICT has worked in over 25 countries on a range of programmes.

For further information please email **ict@training.com**

4 ·))) **5.8** Listen to Karim and Nick comparing the options available and complete their notes.

	Mohammed	British Society Dubai	ICT
Positives	Good that he works in the [1] company	Know about the differences [5] between the two cultures [6]	Professional website and experienced [8]
	Can be very entertaining and funny [2] Like a comedian		Knowledge of the middle [9] ast and the UK
Negatives	Uses PowerPoint [3] too much Might not know much about UK [4]	Not very culturally [7] sensitive?	Very expensive [10].

5 Discuss with a partner which speaker you think would be best and why.

6 Nick sends the speaker an outline of the topics they would like covered. Think of four or five points you would want covered on each slide.

What to do	**Working week**	**Local customs**

Local laws	**Keeping in touch with home**	**Where to shop**

7 What other slides would you add?

8 Imagine someone is coming to your city for work. Prepare a short presentation using the outline from **6** and **7**.

Writing emails

1 Passing on a telephone message

Read the emails. Complete the sentences using the names in the box.

Amélie	Erhan	Hiroko	Luana	Paco

1 .... is taking Paco's calls.
2 .... is having difficulties.
3 .... is running some training.
4 .... is contactable at home.
5 .... is setting up meetings for Paco.
6 .... is preparing for a trade show.
7 .... is organising travel arrangements.
8 .... is back at work after taking time off.

To: luanaf@graftonhall.com
From: pacop@graftonhall.com
Subject: training this week

Hi Luana
Welcome back – hope you had a great holiday.
I'm running a training course this week, so I can't answer calls or emails in work time. Could you email me any important phone messages please, so that I can deal with them in the evening?
Thanks
Paco

To: pacop@graftonhall.com
From: luanaf@graftonhall.com
Subject: re: training this week

Hi Paco
I had a great break, thanks. Hope the training's going well. So, here are the main messages:
• Hiroko called. She's setting up our exhibition at the Tokyo trade fair, but she's having problems. She thinks you can help, and wants you to call her.
• Erhan called. He wants to talk to you about something that's happening in China at the moment – he thinks it could be a good opportunity to break into the market. He's working from home this week and wants you to call him as soon as you're free.
• Amélie called to say she's planning your Brussels trip at the moment. She wants to know if you're planning to visit any suppliers when you're there.
That's it for now. Let me know if you need anything, and good luck for tomorrow.
Luana

Focus on ... the parts of an email

Number the parts of an email in the order they would normally appear:

a greeting
b closing
c sender
d signature
e recipient
f main body
g subject line
h signoff
i opening

Style tip

Here are some ways to start and finish emails to make them sound friendly:

Hope you had a good holiday/trip.
Hope the conference is going well.
Good luck with the presentation tomorrow.

Hope the presentation goes well tomorrow.
Note: Use *I hope* ... in more formal emails:
I hope you had a good holiday.

Language tip

Some verbs are not generally used in the present continuous. Some common ones are:

want	~~She's wanting~~ you to call her.	She wants you to call her.
think	~~She's thinking~~ you can help.	She thinks you can help.
need	~~He's needing~~ to speak to you.	He needs to speak to you.
understand	~~She's understanding~~ your problem.	She understands your problem.
depend on	~~It's depending~~ on the price.	It depends on the price.

›››PHRASEBANK PAGE 54

Task

You're taking calls for your colleague, Ariane, who's at a conference this week. Email her to tell her who called and what they said, using your notes on the right. Use expressions from this page or from the Phrasebank to help you.

Daisuke Tanaka (Japan office) – problems with files you sent (can't open) – please resend
Ellen Moores – visiting this week – meeting possible? – call her ASAP

2 Reporting a technical problem

Read the email and decide if sentences 1–5 are true (T) or false (F).

1 Sari can't open an important email.
2 Her computer wouldn't turn on this morning.
3 She managed to save her report yesterday.
4 She kept getting error messages today.
5 The report won't open now.

To: matt.kray@deltascan.com
From: sari.litmanen@deltascan.com
Subject: pc problems

Hello Matt

I called you, but you were in a meeting, so I'm emailing to catch you before going home. My computer went wrong this morning, and I lost some important work.

The problems actually started yesterday – the screen froze when I was writing a report. I switched the computer off and on and the document saved OK.

This morning, I was trying to send an email, but I kept getting a 'Network error' warning on my screen. I rebooted and there was still something wrong with it – when I tried to save the report again later, the program wouldn't respond.

I got another error message, so I turned off the PC. When I switched it back on, however, the report file wouldn't open and another error message said the file was corrupted. I really hope I can recover this important report!

I'd really appreciate your urgent help with this problem, as I need to finish this work.

I'll be in the office from 8 a.m. tomorrow.

Best
Sari

Focus on ... points to remember

Match the points a–h with the three parts of an email.

subject line   ____
greeting   ____
signoff   ____

a Use *Hi / Hello* in an informal email or when you don't know the name of the person.
b *Best wishes* or *Regards* are often used before the name at the end of a neutral email.
c Make sure it shows the content of the email.
d In an informal or neutral email, *Hi John / Hello John* is the most common way to begin.
e You can end a very informal email with *Cheers* and then your name, or just with your initial.
f *Dear Mr Jones* would be used to start a formal email.
g If you forward an email, it may be useful to change this.
h In an informal email, you can end with *Best* and then your name, or just with your name.

Style tip

Your emails will sound more natural if you join ideas together using 'linking' words. Linking words show the relationship between two ideas:

ACTION/SITUATION ⟶ 'NORMAL' RESULT
*My computer went wrong this morning **and** I lost some work.*
*I got an error message, **so** I turned off the PC.*
'NORMAL' RESULT ⟶ ACTION/SITUATION
*I turned off the PC **because** I got an error message.*
*I would really appreciate your help **as** I need to finish this work.*
ACTION/SITUATION ⟶ UNEXPECTED RESULT
*I called you, **but** you were in a meeting.*

Language tip

If a machine repeatedly does an action you don't want, you can use **keep ... -ing**:

now	*The screen keeps freezing.*
	I keep getting an error message.
earlier	*The screen kept freezing.*
	I kept getting an error message.

If a machine doesn't do an action you want, you can use **won't ... infinitive**:

now	*The file won't open.*
	The program won't respond.
earlier	*The file wouldn't open.*
	The program wouldn't respond.

Task

You've had serious computer problems. Email the IT technician, Jonas Elberg, to tell him about the problems, using the notes on the right. Use expressions from this page or from the Phrasebank to help you.

yesterday / memory stick / not work
files / not open
'corrupt' message
reboot ⟶ some files / open
please help

⟩⟩ PHRASEBANK PAGE 54

3 Enquiring about a product

Read the emails and decide if sentences 1–5 are true (T) or false (F).

1 Mark works for an advertising company.
2 The company needs a colour printer for its new offices.
3 Mark wants to compare the size of different printers.
4 He needs to know what happens if a printer stops working.
5 A lot of people will use the new printers.

To: blackieb@kankandesign.com
From: heimerm@kankandesign.com
Subject: need printer info

Hi Becky
I'm meeting Sam tomorrow to discuss what make and model of printer to get for our new offices. I have heard the new Stonemark PF50 is fantastic, but their website is down. Can you contact them and get some info, please?
Ask how much it costs, obviously, and how much toner* is. Find out how fast it can print 10 photo-quality A4 images, so that we can compare it with other models. Also, we need to know if it's suitable for heavy use as it's a busy office. Check how long the guarantee is, too, and whether it covers all maintenance costs. And, of course, ask when it will be available.
If you could email me the information by 10 tomorrow, that would be great.
Mark

*toner = ink in the form of powder that printers use

To: info@stonemark.com
From: blackieb@kankandesign.com
Subject: PF50 info

Hello
We are a design company, and we are interested in the new PF50. Please could you give me the following details on this model:
- How much does it cost?
- How much is toner?
- How fast can it print 10 photo-quality A4 images?
- How long is the guarantee? Does it cover all maintenance costs?
- Is it suitable for heavy use?
- When will it be available?
I'd be very grateful if you could send me this information by the end of the day, and could you also send me your latest catalogue?
Thank you in advance.
Becky
Rebecca Blackie
Kan-Kan Design Ltd

Focus on ... giving the context

When you send the first email of a conversation, you usually begin (often after a friendly opening) by explaining your situation, so that the recipient understands why you're writing. Here are some examples:

I'm running a training course this week, so ...
I'm having problems with my computer.
I'm meeting Sam tomorrow to discuss ...
A sales rep is visiting from Takeda today.
I'm doing my presentation next week, so ...

Style tip

If you have a list of things you need to ask or tell someone, the clearest way to do so is to use a **numbered list** or **bullet points**:

Please can you give me the following information:
1 *How much does it cost?*
2 *How fast can it print?*
3 *Is it suitable for heavy use?*
Please can you tell me:
- *how much it costs.*
- *how fast it can print.*
- *if it's suitable for heavy use.*

Language tip

When asking for information, we usually use a question form. In more formal contexts we often start with a verb such as *ask, find out, know, check, tell,* etc. When you do this, you do not need to use a question form:

Question form	No question form needed
How much does it cost?	*Ask how much it costs.*
How fast can it print?	*Find out how fast it can print.*
Is it suitable for heavy use?	*We need to know if it's suitable for heavy use.*
How long is the guarantee?	*Check how long the guarantee is.*
Does it cover all labour costs?	*Can you tell me* whether/if it covers all labour costs?*

*Note that *Can you tell me* is a question form, but the main part of the sentence is not.

》》》PHRASEBANK PAGE 5

Task

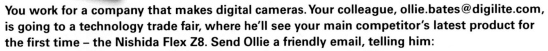

You work for a company that makes digital cameras. Your colleague, ollie.bates@digilite.com, is going to a technology trade fair, where he'll see your main competitor's latest product for the first time – the Nishida Flex Z8. Send Ollie a friendly email, telling him:

- why you can't go to the trade fair.
- what you need to know about the camera:
  - cost • size • weight • number of megapixels • speed • what memory card • type of batteries • when on sale
- when and how to contact you.

Use expressions from this page or from the Phrasebank to help you.

4 Reporting on progress

Read the emails. Tick (✓) the things on Will's 'to-do' list that he has done and cross (✗) the things that he hasn't done yet.

to do:
1 *send out questionnaire*
2 *get questionnaire back*
3 *collect data*
4 *analyse data*
5 *write final version report*
6 *edit report*
7 *print report*
8 *prepare PowerPoint*

To: william.hamlyn@bibliopus.com
From: renate.weber@bibliopus.com
Subject: update

Hi Will
I'm doing my presentation next week, so I just wanted to check how you're doing with the report.
How are you getting on? How far have you got with it? How long will it take you to finish? Don't forget I'll need it by Friday at the latest. Can you give me a quick update, please?
Thanks
Renate

To: renate.weber@bibliopus.com
From: william.hamlyn@bibliopus.com
Subject: re: update

Hi Renate
Don't worry, it's all going fine. I sent out the questionnaire a couple of weeks ago, and I got the last one back yesterday, so now I've got the data together and I've analysed it. So far I've written a quick first version of the report, but I haven't edited it yet. I haven't started working on the PowerPoint slides yet, but they won't take too long. Now I just need to edit the report, do the slides and print everything. I should get it to you tomorrow afternoon. Hope that's OK.
Will

To: william.hamlyn@bibliopus.com
From: renate.weber@bibliopus.com
Subject: re: update

Thanks, Will – that's perfect. Look forward to reading it.
Renate

Focus on ... recipients

When you send the first email of a conversation, your aim is often to ask the recipient to do something, or to ask him/her for information. This request can be near the beginning, after you explain the context or at the end of the message. Here are some examples:

Could you email me any important phone messages, please?

I'd really appreciate your urgent help with this problem.

If you could email me the information by 10.00 tomorrow, that would be great.

I'd be very grateful if you could send me this information by the end of the day.

Please could you also send me your latest catalogue?

Can you give me a quick update, please?

Style tip

Notice how Will invites his boss to confirm that she's happy with his progress:
Hope that's OK.
Quick ways to respond to this could be:
That's great – thanks.
That sounds fine.

Language tip

Some useful phrases for asking about progress are:
How are you getting on (with ...)?
How far have you got (with ...)?
How long will it take (you) (to finish ...)?
When will it be finished?

Useful phrases for reporting on progress are:
It's going fine.
So far I've ..., but I haven't ... yet.
I've done about 30%/80%, etc. so far.
I've got as far as ... ing.
Now I just need to ...

〉〉〉PHRASEBANK PAGE 54

Task

You're preparing for a presentation at a sales conference. Your boss, jenny.chen@martex.com, has asked you how you're getting on. Email her a progress report, using the 'to-do' list on the right. Let her know when you'll finish. Use expressions from this page or from the Phrasebank to help you.

to do:
interview data ✓
spreadsheet ✓
analyse ✓
draft report ✓
final report ✗
discuss with Sarah ✗
write presentation ✗
make PowerPoint slides ✗

5 Giving advice

Read the emails and decide if sentences 1–5 are true (T) or false (F).

1 Rocío is visiting Japan next week for pleasure.
2 John recommends a seafood restaurant.
3 He suggests going to a bath house before it gets busy.
4 He recommends visiting the castle in Osaka.
5 He mentions an example of impolite behaviour in Japan.

To: jpeterson@sternauto.com
From: rrojas@sternauto.com
Subject: Osaka tips?

Hi John
I'm going to Osaka next week and I should have at least one day free. I hear you've been there several times. Do you have any suggestions for what I should do when I'm there?
Thanks
Rocío

To: rrojas@sternauto.com
From: jpeterson@sternauto.com
Subject: re: Osaka tips?

Hi Rocío
So, you're going to Japan. You lucky thing!
You must try the street food when you're there – it's fantastic! As for restaurants, I'd recommend eating at the seafood restaurant with the enormous model crab on the front.
You should also go for a bath at an onsen if you can. It's best to go late afternoon, because it can get quite busy later.
If you have time, you should try and visit Kyoto – it shows you the traditional old Japan, and is well worth a visit. As you're only there for a short time, I wouldn't go to Osaka Castle if I were you, unless you're really into history.
As it's your first time doing business in Japan, maybe it's worth looking up some dos and don'ts on the Internet. One piece of advice from me is don't blow your nose in public, as it's considered very rude.
Anyway, have a great trip, and let me know how you get on.
All the best
John

Focus on ... using paragraphs

If your email contains several ideas, it helps the reader if you break it into paragraphs. In the emails above, Rocío's is short and simple, so she doesn't use paragraphs. John, however, separates the different ideas in his longer email into paragraphs to make it clearer for Rocío. The themes of his six paragraphs are:

friendly opening / food / bath / places to visit / culture / friendly ending

A more typical business email could be divided up into:

friendly greeting / reason for writing / details / request for action or information / friendly ending

Style tip

Notice how Rocío closes her email with *Thanks*. This is a common way to end a message in which you ask for a small favour. For a bigger favour, you can end with *Thanks in advance*:

I'm afraid I can't find the information you sent me. Would you mind resending it?
Thanks in advance
Julia

Language tip

The simplest way to give advice is to use *should*:
You should try and visit Kyoto.
For strongly recommending an experience or a place, you can use *must*:
You must try the street food.
Note: It's best not to use *must* for other advice or instructions, because it's too strong: *You ~~must~~ should / will need to wear warm clothes.*

Here are some other useful phrases for making recommendations:
I'd recommend eating at a crab restaurant.
It's best to go late afternoon.
Nara **is well worth** a visit.
I'd go / I wouldn't go to the castle **if I were you**.
Maybe **it's worth** looking up some dos and don'ts.

Task

>>>PHRASEBANK PAGE 54

A business colleague, josh.stevens@kpp.com, has emailed you to say he's going to a city in your country on business, and he has 24 hours free for sightseeing. Email him with your recommendations. Include:

- a good place to eat
- a place to wander around
- something not to do.
- a historical place
- an activity

Use expressions from this page or from the Phrasebank to help you.

6 Complaining about an order

Read the emails and decide if sentences 1–5 are true (T) or false (F).

1 Gunnar is ordering furniture for the office.
2 Lasse's office has a new computer system.
3 Lasse's company has supplied Gunnar's for years.
4 Gunnar receives shipment about two weeks after ordering.
5 Gunnar refuses to return the incorrect items.

Gunnar Stromberg to customerservice@applo.se
16 May 10:23

I ordered some office stationery 10 days ago, but I haven't received it yet. Can you please check what has gone wrong? My order number is 28287364.
Gunnar Stromberg

---

customerservice@applo.se to Gunnar Stromberg
16 May 11:06

Hello Gunnar
Your order has been shipped now. I'm very sorry there has been a problem. We've just changed our computer system, and we have been having a few problems with orders.
Best wishes
Lasse Maikonen

Gunnar Stromberg to customerservice@applo.se
20 May 16:41

Lasse
My stationery still hasn't arrived. Now I've been waiting for two weeks! We have been ordering from you for several years, and this is not the level of service I expect. Sorry, but unless I receive the order in 24 hours, I'll have to cancel my order.
Gunnar

---

customerservice@applo.se to Gunnar Stromberg
21 May 09:28

Please accept my apologies, Gunnar – our computer system has been down. I have just personally shipped your order by special courier, and it will arrive today.
Lasse

To: customerservice@applo.se
From: gunnars@dedikat.com
Subject: re: order not arrived
21 May 13:32

Lasse
The package has just arrived, but there are some things we didn't order and some items missing. I'm afraid this is not good enough, and I have no option but to cancel my order. Please refund the payment to our account. I will send the unwanted items back to you if you include postage.
Gunnar

Focus on ... avoiding rudeness

If someone is angry on the phone, the listener may slowly forget about it once the conversation has ended. Emails are different – any angry or rude language will stay in the person's inbox, or can be forwarded for others to see. Angry emails can destroy a business relationship, or seriously damage a person's reputation. The key points to remember are:

- Never send an email when you're angry.
- When you complain or criticise, 'soften' the language if you want to keep the relationship (see Style tips for examples).

Be careful when using humour. Remember that the recipient can't see your face and it may not be obvious that you're joking.

Style tip

Notice how Gunnar, although he's angry, still uses some expressions to soften his message:
~~This is terrible service!~~
... **this is not** the level of service **I expect**.
~~This is not good enough, and I'm cancelling my order.~~
I'm afraid this is not good enough, and **I have no option but to** cancel my order.
~~Unless I receive the order in 24 hours, I'll cancel my order.~~
Sorry, but unless I receive the order in 24 hours, **I'll have to** cancel my order.

Language tip

Single action:
use **present perfect simple**.
I **haven't received** it yet.
My stationery still **hasn't arrived**.
Can you please check what **has gone** wrong?
Your order **has been shipped** now.
The package **has** just **arrived**.
I'm very sorry there **has been** a problem.
We **have** just **changed** our computer system.

Repeated or continuous action:
use **present perfect continuous**.
Now I**'ve been waiting** for two weeks!
Both forms possible with little change in meaning.
We **have had / been having** a few problems with orders.
We **have ordered / been ordering** from you for several years.

》》》PHRASEBANK PAGE 54

Task

You ordered office supplies, but there has been a problem with the order. Use the details below to write an email to complain. You decide what action you will take. Use expressions from this page or from the Phrasebank to help you.

Your supplier
- info@kopykwik.com
- 24-hour delivery
- 5 years with no problems

Your order
- photocopier toner and paper
- order placed a week ago
- arrived this morning
- missing and incorrect items

7 Correcting mistakes

Read the emails and decide if sentences 1–5 are true (T) or false (F).

1. Kristel's email is about a meat product.
2. A lot of words are spelled wrongly on the packaging.
3. She can't deal with the problem because she's in a meeting.
4. Paul left a message with the translation agency before replying to Kristel.
5. They've never had problems with translations before.

From: steiner.kristel@barthesfoods.be
To: duclos.paul@barthesfoods.be
Subject: packaging mistake – important!

Paul

This is urgent. I've discovered a serious mistake in the cooking instructions on the chicken pie packaging – the Italian version says 'cook for 4 minutes' instead of 'cook for 40 minutes', which could be dangerous. It's also full of spelling mistakes. We need to correct this before it's printed tomorrow, and check all the translations in case there are more mistakes. I'm leaving for the airport in ten minutes, so I can't help, unfortunately. It's vital that we sort this out before it's printed, so please do this ASAP.
Kristel

From: duclos.paul@barthesfoods.be
To: steiner.kristel@barthesfoods.be
Subject: re: packaging mistake – important!

Kristel
Well done for finding the mistakes! I'll call the printers as soon as they open tomorrow morning – I've already emailed and left a voicemail, but I'll make sure I speak to the manager in person.
I'll contact the translation agency, and I'm sure they'll be able to check all the translations in a couple of hours.
This isn't the first time we've had problems with the translations, so I'm going to bring it up at the next department meeting. We'll talk about how we can avoid this happening again.
So don't worry, enjoy your trip, and I'll let you know what happens.
Paul

Focus on ... improving your email language

Here are two tips to help you keep improving your email language:

- Cut and paste useful expressions from emails you receive into a document.
- If you write a phrase, and you're not sure it's accurate, type it into an internet search engine in double quotes (" "). If it's correct, there will be a very large number of hits.

Style tip

Notice how Paul uses positive language to reassure Kristel that he's dealing with the problem, and to help her not to worry:

Well done for finding the mistakes!
I've already emailed and left a voicemail, but ***I'll make sure*** I speak to the manager in person.
... ***I'm sure they'll be able to*** check all the translations in a couple of hours.
We'll talk about how we can ***avoid this happening*** again.
So don't worry, enjoy your trip, and ***I'll let you know*** what happens.

Language tip

A new situation often requires instant decisions. We usually express these decisions with ***I'll ...*** (= I will / shall ...):

I'll call the printers.
I'll make sure I speak to the manager in person.
I'll contact the translation agency.

After we've had time to think about a decision, we often change from ***I'll ...*** to ***I'm going to ...***:

I'm going to bring it up at the next meeting.

〉〉〉PHRASEBANK PAGE 55

Task

It's a big day – your company is launching an important new product. Unfortunately, you have just looked at the website, and the picture is wrong – it shows a competitor's product! Send an urgent email to your boss, marek.baranski@techpro.com. Tell him what action you will take involving the following people:

Taro (in charge of the website)   Claudia (in charge of product photos)   Bill (Marketing Manager – meeting next week)

Use expressions from this page or from the Phrasebank to help you.

8 Making a difficult request

Read the emails. Complete the sentences using the names in the box.

Carmen	Jeff	Mei-li	Piotr

1 .... agrees to a request.
2 .... will communicate with Piotr.
3 .... needs something fixed.
4 .... has the latest designs.
5 .... wants a phone meeting.
6 .... doesn't have any holiday allowance left.

To: jeff.dekoch@ddm.com
From: meili.long@ddm.com
Subject: washing machine problem

Hi Jeff
My washing machine has broken down, and I need to arrange a time for the repair man to come. Unfortunately, I have no holiday allowance left. Would it be possible for me to work from home tomorrow?
Mei-li

To: meili.long@ddm.com
From: jeff.dekoch@ddm.com
Subject: re: washing machine problem

Hi Mei-li
That should be fine as long as you can rearrange any meetings, and everyone's happy with it. It's OK with me though as it's a one-off.
Jeff

To: carmen.vello@ddm.com
From: meili.long@ddm.com
Subject: phone conference?

Hi Carmen
I'm having to work from home today, as my washing machine has broken down. Would you mind if we had the meeting over the phone rather than in person? If that's OK with you, do you think you could set up a phone conference? I don't have Piotr's contact details here, so if you could let him know, I'd be grateful. Also, would you be able to send me the latest designs so that I can look at them before the meeting?
Thanks, and sorry for the hassle.
Mei-li

To: meili.long@ddm.com
From: carmen.vello@ddm.com
Subject: phone conference?

Hi Me-ili
Sorry to hear about your problem. That's fine. I'll let Piotr know and confirm it with you shortly.
Carmen

Focus on ... improving your spelling

Bad spelling in a business email can seem unprofessional. Here are some tips for making sure your spelling is always good.

- Use a dictionary! Keep a file for noting all spellings that surprise you or that you got wrong.
- Use your email program's spell-checker. Be careful, though! – if you accidentally type the wrong word, the spell-checker won't notice it, for example *I'm out **off** the office* instead of *I'm out **of** the office*.

Here are 20 words which native English speakers often spell incorrectly:

accommodation	excellent	recommend
address	foreign	reference
alright	guarantee	referring
commercial	immediately	separate
committee	officially	successful
definitely	questionnaire	unnecessary
equipment	receive	

Style tip

Notice how Jeff doesn't simply agree to Mei-li's request by saying *That's fine*. Instead, he gives cautious agreement using *should*, and adds a condition using *as long as*:

*That **should** be fine **as long as** you can rearrange any meetings, and everyone's happy with it.*

Language tip

When we're making a difficult request, or asking someone for a difficult favour, sometimes basic questions can sound too direct. To sound 'extra polite' in these situations, we sometimes use more complicated grammar:

Would it be possible (for me) **to** work from home tomorrow?
Would you mind if I work**ed** from home tomorrow?
Would you be able to send me the latest designs?
Do you think you could send me the latest designs?
I'd be grateful if you could send me the latest designs.
Is there any way you could send me the latest designs?

>>> PHRASEBANK PAGE 55

Task

You have an important meeting arranged with your boss, linda.marwick@directfinance.com, tomorrow morning. Tomorrow afternoon, you have a meeting arranged with a client, Thomas Heller. Unfortunately, you have just realised that you have an important hospital appointment tomorrow, which will take all day.

Email your boss to tell her this, and (very politely!) ask her to:

- postpone your meeting (suggest possible times)
- contact the client and say you need to rearrange.

Use expressions from this page or from the Phrasebank to help you.

9 Explaining and apologising

Read the emails and decide if sentences 1–6 are true (T) or false (F).

1 The deadline for the report was yesterday.
2 Sandro filed the report in the incorrect folder.
3 He was in a meeting for the whole morning.
4 He noticed his mistake while he was with the Sales Manager.
5 He wrote a first version of the report before seeing the new sales figures.
6 He's going to finish the report by the following morning.

To: sandro.mazzini@centrumpublishing.com
From: mina.kaboul@centrumpublishing.com
Subject: missing report!

Sandro
I had an important meeting with the Sales Manager this morning, but when I looked for the report in the Sales folder, it wasn't there. You were supposed to finish it last week. Did you file it in the wrong place by mistake? I had to rely on my notes in the meeting, and it was a little embarrassing. I called you, but you weren't at your desk all morning.
Mina

To: mina.kaboul@centrumpublishing.com
From: sandro.mazzini@centrumpublishing.com
Subject: re: missing report!

Hi Mina
Sorry I couldn't take your call earlier – I was in a meeting with the designer all morning.
I was looking through my diary during the meeting when I realised I hadn't written the sales report. I'm so sorry about that, especially as this caused you problems in your meeting. I'd written a draft report when we got the latest sales figures last week. I'm afraid I had a backlog of work at the end of the week, and I didn't get round to writing up the final version before the weekend. I'm afraid it just slipped my mind this week. I'll start writing it straight away, and I'll have the report in the Sales folder by first thing tomorrow. I'll also use the calendar on my phone to ensure this doesn't happen again.
Apologies again.
Sandro

Focus on ... punctuation

Here are some tips on using the most common punctuation marks:

- A **full stop** (.) shows where one idea ends and another starts:
  Sorry I missed your call. I have some news for you.
- A **comma** (,) is used in lists, or to join linked ideas:
  I'll be in the office on Monday, Wednesday and Friday.
  I'm so sorry about that, especially as this caused you problems in your meeting.
- A **dash** (–) is used to add an explanation or extra information to a sentence:
  Sorry I couldn't take your call earlier – I was meeting with the designer all morning.
- **Brackets** ( ) are used to add an explanation, comment, etc. to help the reader:
  He wants you to get in touch with him before 10 p.m. today (your time).
- A **colon** (:) is used to show that information comes next:
  Here are the main messages:
  1. Hiroko called …

Style tip

We usually use *sorry* to apologise in informal or neutral language. In more formal writing, *apologies* or *apologise* are more common. Here are some examples:

informal	*Sorry I didn't/couldn't reply earlier.*
	Sorry about that.
neutral	*I'm sorry I didn't/couldn't reply earlier.*
	I'm sorry about that.
formal	*My apologies for not replying earlier.*
	I must apologise for not replying earlier.

Language tip

If you make a mistake, the 'softest' way to present it is to **apologise**, then **explain**, then **say what you'll do** to put the things right. Here are some useful expressions:

Apologise
Sorry I couldn't take your call this morning.
Explain
I'm afraid I had a backlog of work at the end of the week.
Say what you'll do
I'll start writing it straight away (= immediately).

⟩⟩⟩PHRASEBANK PAGE 55

Task

You have just arrived at work. Your first email is from your boss, daniel.desouza@storvac.com, asking where the sales data is. Then you remember ... you had to collect and print sales data for your boss for his meeting tomorrow. You had too much work last week, and forgot! Write an email to Daniel, saying:

- why you missed the deadline
- when you'll finish it
- how you'll avoid similar mistakes in the future.

Use expressions from this page or from the Phrasebank to help you.

10 Sending a notice to staff

Read the email and decide if sentences 1–4 are true (T) or false (F).

1 Someone will take away paper for recycling every day.

2 Confidential papers should not be recycled.

3 Metal waste should be thrown away in the bins by the lifts.

4 There is a document with the email on which staff can write their comments.

To: all staff
From: fcueto@qqpress.com
Subject: new recycling system

To all staff
This is a reminder that a new paper and plastic recycling system is being launched today.
The new green and white bins can be found next to the lifts on all floors.
Waste paper should be put in the green bins, and plastic is collected in the white bins.
The bins will be emptied daily.
Staff are reminded that confidential or sensitive documents should be shredded before being thrown away.
Please note that these bins must not be used for non-paper or plastic waste – please put any other waste in the general bins in your office.
A questionnaire is attached to this email in which you are requested to give feedback on the new system.
Franklin Cueto
Facilities Manager

Focus on formal vs informal language

Official notices use very formal language. Some typical differences between very formal and neutral emails are:

very formal	neutral
Impersonal language	
To all staff	*Dear all*
Staff are reminded that …	*Remember to …*
Frequent use of passive	
A new system is being launched.	*We are launching a new system.*
The bins can be found …	*You can find the bins …*
Formal vocabulary	
You are requested to …	*Please could you …*
Please refrain from putting food waste in these bins.	*Please do not put food waste in these bins.*

Style tip

Official notices can be sent as an **email**, a **memo** or a **circular**. Here are the main differences between these three:

email	memo
• only electronic	• usually printed
• to any number of people	• usually personal
• recipient(s) can send a reply	• reply not expected
• can be formal or informal	• can be formal or informal

circular
• usually electronic   • reply not expected
• to all staff   • usually formal

Language tip

In formal and general instructions, modal verbs such as *can / should / must / will* are often used passively:

modal + *be* + past participle
*The bins **can be found** next to the lifts.*
*Waste paper **should be put** in the green bins.*
*Bins **must** not **be used** for non-paper or plastic waste.*
*The bins **will be emptied** daily.*

》》》PHRASEBANK PAGE 55

Task

From next Monday, your office will have a new desk-sharing system, where people can use any free desk. Send an email to all staff to remind them about this. Use the notes on the right to tell them about the details. Use expressions from this page or from the Phrasebank to help you.

> reminder: Monday launch
> clear desk every evening
> no personal photos
> use locker for personal items
> don't use local computer for documents (use personal folder)
> don't use USB drives to avoid virus problems

Phrasebank

1 Friendly openings: referring to someone's activities

Hope you had a great holiday.
Hope the training / your trip's going well.
Enjoy your evening.
Good luck for tomorrow / with the presentation.

Passing on a message

I have a couple of messages to pass on.
Amélie called (to say ...).

Saying what someone is doing at the moment

I'm running a training course this week.
She's setting up our stand at the trade fair.
They're having some problems with suppliers.
He's working from home at the moment.
She's planning your Brussels trip.
He's meeting suppliers all day today.

Saying why someone called

She thinks you can help / it would be a good opportunity.
She wants to know if ... / what ... / who ..., etc.
He needs to speak to you about prices.
He wants to talk to you about dates.

Saying what action someone wants

She'd like you to call or email her before tomorrow.
He wants you to call him as soon as you're free.
He needs you to get in touch with him before 5 p.m.
Can you call him ASAP (= as soon as possible)?

2 Reporting problems

My computer's gone wrong.
There's something wrong with my email.
My phone isn't working properly.
There's / I've got a problem with my phone.
It won't switch on.
It wouldn't switch on this morning.
It keeps stopping (= repeatedly).
I kept getting an error warning yesterday.

Asking for help

I'd really appreciate your help.
I would really appreciate your urgent help with this problem.
I hope you can help with this.
I hope you'll be able to help me.

Linking actions/situations and results

My computer went wrong this morning, and I lost some work.
I got an error message, so I turned off the PC.
I turned off the PC because I got an error message.
I would really appreciate your help, as I need to finish this work.
I called you, but you were in a meeting.

3 Asking about a product: direct questions

How much is it?
How much does it cost?
How fast can it copy?
Is it suitable for heavy use?

How long is the guarantee?
Does the guarantee cover all maintenance costs?
When will it be available?

Asking about a product: indirect questions

Ask how much toner costs.
Find out how fast it can print.
We need to know if it's suitable for heavy use.
Check how long the guarantee is.
Check whether/if it covers all maintenance costs.
Can you tell me how long the guarantee is?
Do you know when it will be available?

4 Asking about progress

How are you getting on?
How far have you got with it?
How long will it take (you) to finish?
Can you give me a quick update, please?

Reporting on progress

It's all going fine.
I've analysed the data.
I've written the report.
I haven't prepared my presentation yet.
I still haven't printed the handouts.
I still need to print out the report.
I should finish it later today.
I'll get it to you by Friday at the latest.

5 Asking for travel recommendations

Do you have any suggestions for what I should do when I'm there?
Do you have any tips for what to do there?

Making travel recommendations

You should try and visit Kyoto.
You must try the street food.
I'd recommend eating at a seafood restaurant.
It's best to go late afternoon.
Nara is well worth a visit.
I'd go / I wouldn't go to the castle if I were you.
Maybe it's worth looking up some dos and don'ts.

Wishing someone a good trip

Have a great trip/time.
Have a fantastic trip/time.
Enjoy your trip.

6 Saying what the problem is

I ordered some stationery 10 days ago, but I haven't received it yet.
My stationery still hasn't arrived.
You've sent me the wrong items.
There are some wrong/missing items.
The order contains incorrect items.
The order's incomplete.
Now I've been waiting for two weeks!

Complaining

This is not the level of service I expect.
I'm afraid this is not good enough.
I'm very disappointed with this service.

Taking action

Unless I receive the order in 24 hours, I will cancel my order.
I have no option but to cancel my order.
Please refund the payment to our account.

Reassuring the customer

Your order has been shipped now.
I have just personally shipped your order by special courier, and it will arrive today.
Your order should arrive tomorrow.

Apologising

I'm very sorry there has been a problem.
Please accept my apologies.

Explaining the reason for the problem

We've just changed our computer system, and we've been having a few problems with orders.
Our computer system's been down.
We've been short of staff recently.

7 Saying what action is needed

We need to correct this.
It's vital that we sort this out.

Telling someone to act quickly

This is urgent.
Please do this ASAP (= as soon as possible).

Saying what action you will take: deciding now

I'll call the printers as soon as they open.
I'll contact the translation agency.
I'll let you know what happens.

Saying what action you will take: already planned

I'm going to bring it up at the next department meeting.
I'm going to find out how this happened.

8 Making a difficult request

Would it be possible for me to work from home tomorrow?
Would you mind if we had the meeting over the phone rather than in person?
If that's OK with you, do you think you could set up a phone conference?
If you could let him know, I'd be grateful.
Would you be able to send me the latest designs?
Is there any way you could come in just for the meeting?

Agreeing to a request

That's fine.
No problem.
Yes, that should be fine, as long as it's a one-off.

Refusing a request

I'm afraid a phone conference isn't possible, as we're looking at designs.
That won't be possible, I'm afraid, as the video conferencing room isn't available.
It would be very hard to put Piotr off as I know he's very busy next week.

9 Apologising

Sorry I couldn't take your call this morning.
Sorry I missed the meeting yesterday.
I'm so sorry about that.
(at the end of the email:) Apologies again.

Explaining what happened

I'm afraid I had a backlog of work at the end of the week.
I didn't get round to writing up the final version before the weekend.
I'm afraid it just slipped my mind.

Promising action

I'll start writing it straight away (= immediately).
I'll have the report in the Sales folder by first thing tomorrow.
I'll have it on your desk by 5 p.m.
I'll use the calendar on my phone to ensure this doesn't happen again.

10 Reminding people very formally

This is a reminder that a new recycling system will be launched on Monday.
You are reminded that a new recycling system will be launched on Monday.

Giving very formal instructions

Waste paper should be put in the green bins.
Please note that these bins must not be used for non-paper waste.

Start up

1 The Mourtinho family have arrived at the airport to find that the car they hired is not available. Look at the pictures and discuss the questions with a partner.

1. Which car do you think they would be satisfied with as a substitute?
2. Have you ever been offered a substitute product when the product you wanted wasn't available?
3. How do you think it affects customer satisfaction when a product or service has to be substituted?

2 Work with a partner and think about your company. What different products and services does it provide? Who buys each product or service?

Listening

3 ·))) **6.1** Listen to three different customers. What product or service are they calling about?

Customer 1 _Stolen_   Customer 2 _service For computer_   Customer 3 _Information For a trainning cours_

4 Listen again and complete the sentences.

Customer 1: Finally! I _have been trying_ [1] to contact someone all day!
Customer service: _Have you tried_ [2] our website? Most questions can be answered there.
Customer 1: Yes, I _have tried_ [3] it and I've sent five emails, but I _haven't received_ [4] a response.

Customer 2: _I've been having_ [5] problems with my computer all day.
IT services: What seems to be the problem?
Customer 2: It _'s crashed_ [6] twice and the screen _has frozen_ [7] three times.
IT services: _Have you tried_ [8] switching it on and off again?
Customer 2: I've done that five times now.

Mark: Tom, it's Mark here from Eastlight. I still _haven't received_ [9] the information for the training course.
Tom: Really? How long ago did you request it?
Mark: I _'ve been waiting_ [10] for three weeks now and the course starts next week.

Grammar

Present perfect simple and continuous

Use both the present perfect simple and continuous for an activity that started in the past and hasn't finished, sometimes with no difference in meaning.

I've lived here for three years.
I've been living here for three years.

When the focus is on a completed action, use the present perfect simple.

She's written the report and sent it to everyone in the department.

When the focus is on the activity and it may not be finished, use the present perfect continuous.

I've been writing the report all morning but should have finished it by 5pm.

When the focus is on how long, use the present perfect continuous.

I've been waiting for six hours.

More practice

>>>GRAMMAR REFERENCE PAGE 108

5 Complete the sentences.

1 I .... (try) to contact him all week.
2 I .... (already ring) them five times.
3 I .... (learn) English since I was five.
4 This is the first I .... (hear) about the problem.
5 My computer .... (stop) working.
6 The screen .... (break) already.

Reading

6 Read the emails. What have the companies been doing to improve customer service?

a

Our department *has been receiving/has received*[1] a lot of complaints lately. The trouble is our staff are very knowledgeable, but not everyone has the same level of IT knowledge. So for the last month, we *have been encouraging/have encouraged*[2] our staff to be patient with our colleagues. We *have told/have been telling*[3] them to explain simple solutions in a tactful way, and reminded them to be respectful – it might be the CEO on the phone!

b

Many customers *have been complaining/have complained*[4] about how knowledgeable our customer service team are. Well, unknowledgeable really! As a result, we *have changed/have been changing*[5] the organisation of our customer service team. Now, engineers, who are more competent at discussing the products we produce, deal with the more technical complaints.

c

Our sales are all business-to-business and so the contracts can be quite big and important. The difficulty we *have had/have been having*[6] is sales teams making promises they can't keep and not spending the time needed to develop the relationships. We *have been providing/have provided*[7] ongoing training to emphasise the importance of being honest about what we can deliver and being attentive to our clients needs.

7 Choose the correct verb form in *italics*. Sometimes both options are possible.

Vocabulary

8 Complete the sentences with adjectives highlighted in the emails in **6**.

1 Your staff have to be .... of the customer's opinions.
2 I would prefer my team to be .... and tell the customer it was our mistake than to lie.
3 We find out the subject of the customer's complaint first, so that the most .... member of our team in that area speaks to them.
4 He's really .... He takes his time to explain things clearly.
5 It's important to be .... when explaining a customer has made a mistake. We don't want to make them feel bad.
6 Being .... to a customer's needs makes them feel important.
7 Good product knowledge is important in order to be .... in this role.

More practice

Speaking

9 Work with a partner. What qualities do you think are most important for good customer service?

10 Work with a partner. Student A, look at page 97. Student B, look at page 100.

Start up ❶ Look at the methods of measuring customer satisfaction and discuss the questions with a partner.

> discussion forums   focus groups   questionnaires

1 What experience do you have of these as a customer?
2 Which ones does your company use?
3 Does your company use any other methods to check customer satisfaction?

Reading ❷ Read the text and match the headings with the paragraphs.

1 I'm different
2 It all happens online
3 We want it now
4 Hard to please

Generation Y

a .... Born between 1977 and 1994? If so, then you are perhaps the most demanding consumer ever – Generation Y – with very high expectations. Every company has to adapt to their target market, so how do you please Generation Y?

b .... Generation Y have grown up with the Internet, online shopping and 24/7 access to information. They don't want to join the queue or wait on hold, they want answers now! Real-time customer service, with instant responses and resolutions are not what Generation Y hope for – it's what they expect. Even better, don't make Generation Y speak to you. They're happy to find out the answer for themselves.

c .... Internet spending in the UK alone has risen from £2 billion in 2000 to £70 billion in 2011. As a result, an online presence, not only via a website, but through a number of social media, has become increasingly important for any company. It took Facebook two and a half years to grow to ten million users, but it only took Google sixteen days to jump to the same number for its social media site Google+.

d .... But don't put these people into the same group. They don't want to be a group of consumers with the same characteristics; they're individual consumers. They expect services and products to be changed to meet their needs. Use your technology to personalise their experience and you might just make the least loyal consumer in history stay with you.

❸ Replace the word or phrase in *italics* with the correct form of a highlighted word from the text.

1 A *typical quality* of Generation Y is that they want everything now.
2 You have to adapt to the *group of people you want to sell to*.
3 It's my belief that customer service should be *adapted to each individual*.
4 *Regular and unchanging* customers are important to keep.
5 Our customers have the *belief* that we should change to meet their needs.
6 Generation Y customers are *in need of a lot of time and attention*.

Vocabulary 4 Which paragraph in the reading text describes change? <u>Underline</u> words or phrases that show how things are changing.

5 Complete the sentences using the prepositions in the box.

| at   between   by (x2)   from   to (x2)   up |

More practice

1 Last year car sales decreased ....by...... 15%.
2 Since Amazon launched in 1995, Internet spending in the UK has increased ......from...... less than £100 million ......to........ more than £70 billion per year.
3 In 2011, the number of tweets per day jumped .....to........ an average of 140 million.
4 Money spent on TV advertising in the UK has fluctuated .....between. £3.7 and £4.1 billion per year.
5 The number of people using Google+ shot .....up.......... to ten million in just sixteen days.
6 Amazon's revenue now stands ....at....... over $35 billion dollars per year.
7 Customer loyalty has plummeted ....by........ 40% in two generations.

Listening 6 �))) 6.2 Listen to a marketing manager talking about changes they've made to their customer service in response to Generation Y. What are the three main changes?

Change 1 ....
Change 2 ....
Change 3 ....

7 Complete the descriptions of the graphs described in 6 using vocabulary from 5.

1

... especially Twitter, which ...increased its number of tweets per day very slowly ...from... 2007 ...to... January 2009 ...to... one million. In the next year, it ...shot... ...up... to nearly 50 million per day.

2

Customer loyalty for people born before 1929 was high at just over 55%. This ...increased gradually ...to... 57% for war babies and then ...fell... slightly for the baby boomers back ...to... 55%. This then ...decreased... ...to... 50% for Generation X and then ...plummeted ...to... nearly 40% for Generation Y.

3

Our sales online ...increase by... one million every year for the first three years and then ...jumped by... five million every year after that and now stand at thirteen million per year.

8 Listen again and check your answers.

Speaking 9 Student A, look at the graph on page 98. Student B, look at the graph on page 100. Use language from this lesson to describe your graph to your partner. Draw the graph your partner describes.

? Trends are often described with either the past simple or the present perfect simple/continuous. We use the present perfect when the trend is connected to now.

Start up **1** Look at the pictures and discuss with a partner why each person isn't happy.

2 Have you complained about any of these things recently? Tell your partner about it.

Reading **3** Discuss the questions with a partner.

1 Have you ever complained publicly using social media such as Twitter or Facebook?
2 What do you think are the advantages of social media for a customer?
3 How do you think a company should handle such public complaints?

4 Read the text and answer the questions.

1 Why did Chris complain?
2 Was his problem solved by the reception desk?
3 How did he get the problem solved?

Complaining on Twitter

Twitter is a powerful platform for complaining. Thanks to Twitter, the 'little guy' isn't quite so little any more. These days, businesses receive public feedback whether they want it or not and different companies deal with this reality in different ways. Last October, Chris was in Chicago for a few days attending a communications seminar. Unfortunately, close to midnight, a group of teenagers started making a lot of noise. When Chris complained, a security guard came up and it became calm. However, it soon started again. The next morning, the desk clerks simply said they would notify the manager.

So Chris started tweeting. Very quickly the manager of the hotel was on the phone saying that a manager from the New York office wanted her to do whatever she could to fix the situation. His whole stay was free and he was moved into the Executive Suite for the rest of his visit.

Best practices for consumers complaining on Twitter

1 Be responsible and don't overdo it.
2 Express genuine frustration, but don't use bad language.
3 Mention the corporate Twitter account.
4 Go as high up the company as possible.
5 Include photos or video (if applicable) to prove your point.
6 When an issue is resolved, thank the company publicly.

Best practices for companies dealing with complaints on Twitter

1 Employ social media monitoring software to follow brand conversations.
2 Respond to complaints quickly.
3 Check that a person is a real customer before taking action.
4 Go above and beyond the call of duty – even if a person has a small following, people can easily search keywords related to your brand.
5 Once an issue has been resolved, ask the customer if they were satisfied and if they could tweet about it.

If you're a consumer and you have a Twitter account, don't be afraid to do a little public complaining from time to time using the rules above. You really have nothing to lose.

5 Read the text again. Are the sentences true or false?

1 Tweeting lots, and about anything, is a good way to complain. F
2 Tweet the head office if possible. T
3 Don't worry about customer tweets – no one pays any attention. F
4 Do as little as possible when solving the problem. T
5 Ask customers to tweet about good service. T

Listening

6 ·))) 6.3 Listen to three different complaints. What is the product and why is each customer not happy?

1 Product *Jard oz brochur* . Unhappy because *1600*
2 Product *fotocopier* . Unhappy because *The paper is stuck*
3 Product *computer* Unhappy because *It keeps crashing* *, doen't have interuct*

7 Listen again and complete the phrases.

M 1 Unfortunately, *there's a problm with* the order you sent.
D 2 Sorry to *hear that* . What's the *problem* ?
D 3 I can see it's *our mistake* .
M 4 We have a photocopier on hire from you and *the paper keeps* getting stuck.
D 5 I think we'll *have sent* out an engineer.
D 6 *I'm sorry abt* the delay.
M 7 It's *my computer* – it keeps crashing
M 8 *Can you explain* when and how?
D 9 *Have you tried* switching it on and off again?
10 *thinck you should* check that and then get back to me if it still doesn't work.

8 Which phrases in **7** are used to make a complaint and which are used to deal with the complaint?

Say it right 9 ·))) 6.4 Look at the dialogue on page 123. Listen to the first customer again and underline any words that are stressed strongly.

10 Tell a partner why you think these words were stressed. Listen again and practise stressing the words.

Speaking

11 Student A, look at the situation below. Student B, look at page 97. Role play the situation.

You've taken an important client out for dinner and are not happy with a number of things.
• overcooked food
• rude service
• slow service

Complain to the manager. You want an apology and a discount.

Writing

12 Work with a partner. Student A, look below. Student B, look at page 96.

Write a tweet complaining about your mobile phone's poor service.
Tweet that your phone can't receive calls.
Tweet that you have tried four times, but have to wait too long for an answer.
Tweet your satisfaction with the response.

Scenario: How rude!

1 Elba is a mobile phone sales company. They also provide aftersales care to maintain and repair the equipment they sell. They want to check the standard of their customer service and have created a questionnaire. Think of the mobile phone company that you use and complete the questionnaire.

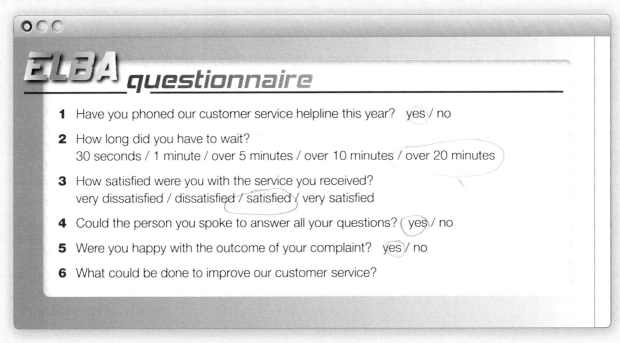

ELBA *questionnaire*

1 Have you phoned our customer service helpline this year? yes / no

2 How long did you have to wait?
30 seconds / 1 minute / over 5 minutes / over 10 minutes / over 20 minutes

3 How satisfied were you with the service you received?
very dissatisfied / dissatisfied / satisfied / very satisfied

4 Could the person you spoke to answer all your questions? yes / no

5 Were you happy with the outcome of your complaint? yes / no

6 What could be done to improve our customer service?

2 Show your results to a partner and explain the reasons for your answers.

3 Work with a partner. Student A, look at the bar charts below for Elba's customers' responses to questions 1 and 2. Student B, look at the bar charts on page 98 for Elba's customers' responses to questions 3 and 4. Describe your bar charts to your partner so that you have a complete set.

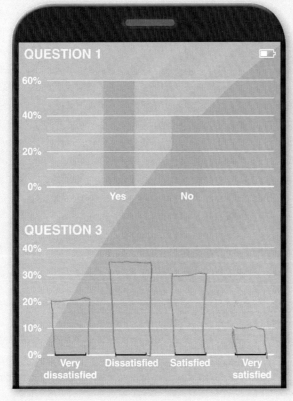

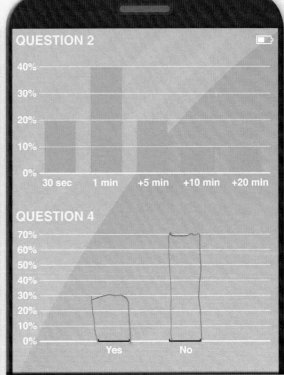

④ Plot the results for this year (year 5) on to the graphs below.

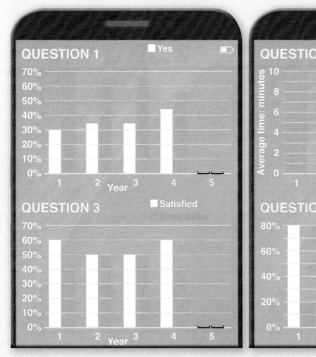

⑤ ◖)) **6.5** Listen to Monica and Lukas discussing questions 5 and 6 in ① and complete the graphs.

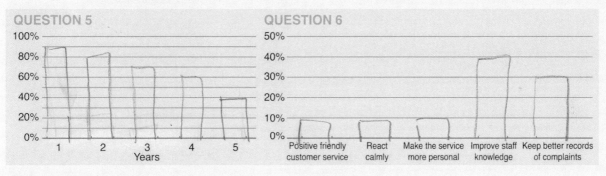

⑥ Discuss with a partner what you think the main problems are and what the company can do to improve their customer service.

⑦ ◖)) **6.6** The company have decided to monitor calls to improve service. Listen to two calls and complete the assessment log.

Does the Customer Service Representative …	Paloma	Tomas
answer the phone within three rings?	✗	✓
greet the customer in a friendly way?	✓	✗
give their own name?	✓	✗
give the company name?	✗	✗
stay calm and listen?	✗	✗
show empathy?	✗	✗

⑧ Work with a partner and discuss the different things their staff are doing wrong. Write an email for all staff with recommendations for handling calls in general and specifically complaints.

7 The future of work
Making predictions
will and *be going to*

ma'am

Start up

1 Look at the pictures and describe what changes have happened.

2 How will each thing in the pictures change in the next twenty years?

Reading

3 Read the text. Who is Faith Popcorn and what does her company do?

The end of gender

Faith Popcorn is a futurist, author, and founder and CEO of marketing consulting firm Faith Popcorn's BrainReserve. By watching and listening to events in the world, they spot trends and connections to predict future events.

Every year BrainReserve makes annual predictions. In 2011, the predictions were called The year of EN-GEN – the end of gender. They reported that the USA will not be divided into male and female, just human. Women are becoming more influential and powerful – women now hold 51% of managerial or professional positions and four in ten mothers are a household's main earner. Also single, childless women earn more than their male peers. Men's roles are changing as well. There was a 62% increase in stay-at-home dads between 2003 and 2008 and a 40% increase in male time spent doing housework. So what does this all mean for the future?

There will be fewer male-dominated jobs like construction and manufacturing and more employment in female sectors such as education, healthcare and social services. Confused, unemployed, undereducated men will have to adapt to this woman-friendly world. One economist predicts that if they don't, they won't be needed any more. So what trends are there that point to this change?

1 Products will not have a typical male or female design. For example, Apple and Nespresso are just stylish neutral designs.

2 Hobbies and interests will change. In Japan, flower arranging is already a popular hobby for men and Japan is a country where many trends start.

3 Female values such as environmentalism and concern for the world will mean an increase in sales of electric cars.

4 A difficult economy will mean it's harder for older men to get work and there will be an increase in cosmetic surgery for men.

5 Increased concern about where food and products come from will mean more people buying vegan-friendly products.

? vegan – someone who doesn't eat any animal products

(4) Read the text again and answer the questions.

1 What was BrainReserve's main prediction for 2011?
2 What positions do women now hold over half of?
3 What jobs will there be fewer of and what will there be more of?
4 What hobby is becoming popular with men in Japan?
5 Why will cosmetic surgery become more popular with men?

(5) Discuss the questions with a partner.

1 Which of the five trends are happening in your country?
2 Do you think the world is becoming more female/feminine?
3 Do you think men and women's roles are changing in your country?

Listening

(6) ·))) 7.1 Listen to two people discussing the predictions. Tick (✓) whether they think the predictions from the text are likely or unlikely.

Maria
1	likely ✓	unlikely
2	likely ✓	unlikely
3	likely ✓	unlikely
4	likely ✓	unlikely
5	likely	unlikely ✓

Carlos
likely ✓	unlikely
likely	unlikely ✓
likely ✓	unlikely
likely	unlikely ✓
likely ✓	unlikely

(7) Listen again and complete the sentences.

1 I agree that people are still _going to_ buy products and need offices and places to live.
2 People _are going_ to buy different products.
3 You might not, but some men _will_ .
4 I think it's _going_ to change because it has to. We can't rely on petrol.
5 True, it probably _will_ happen, but not for a long time.
6 Ninety per cent of any menu is still meat or fish. People are _few_ eat meat for a long time yet.
7 Maybe, but people _will_ start to eat more vegetarian meals.

(8) Which predictions in **(7)** are the speakers more confident will happen?

Grammar

(9) Read the rules below and check your answer to **(8)**.

***will* and *be going to* – predictions**

Be going to is often used when we have strong evidence in the present and is used more commonly for predictions for the immediate future.

90% of any menu is still meat or fish. People are going to eat meat for a long time yet.

Will is used to make predictions based more on personal opinion or feelings.

I think it will, but only a few people will do it.

》》GRAMMAR REFERENCE PAGE 109

(10) Complete the sentences using *will* or *be going to*. Sometimes both are correct

1 The company has been taken over. The last time this happened, a lot of people lost their jobs. I think there _are going to_ be job cuts.
2 It's four o'clock and they're still working on the project. They _aren't going to_ finish it.
3 People _will_ eat less meat if it becomes more expensive.
4 Have you seen the sales figures? There _going to_ be trouble!
5 She _will_ leave. What makes you say that? I don't know, it's just a feeling.
6 The government keep increasing the retirement age. People _are going to_ work until they are 80.

More practice

Speaking

(11) Work with a partner and discuss your predictions for your own company or sector. Try to make predictions with both *will* and *be going to*.

Start up ① Work with a partner. Discuss which of these you think are easiest to improve. How can you do it?

efficiency   memory and concentration   time management

Listening ② ·))) 7.2 GloCo is an energy company that is having a number of organisational problems. Listen to three meetings. What skill or ability from ① needs to be improved in each?

Meeting 1 *efficiency*
Meeting 2 *time management*
Meeting 3 *memory*

Reading ③ Read the article on time management and match the headings 1–3 with paragraphs a–c.

1 Efficiency
2 Time management
3 Memory and concentration

Work smarter, not harder

Few people enjoy working long hours, but bosses often want us to work more. How can you work less but keep your boss happy?

a *Efficiency*

Make lists of things you're going to do, but keep the list small. When the list is big, make it smaller by dividing it into a number of lists. You then get a sense of achievement by completing each small list. When you're walking, driving or showering, prioritise your goals for the day. Few people like deadlines as they cause stress and worry. Unfortunately, your boss usually sets the deadlines, so take control and decide when you're going to do the work before the deadline.

b *Memory and Concentration*

Exercising the body exercises the brain. Treating your body well can enhance your ability to process and recall information. Make sure you get good sleep. A lack of sleep means your brain can't operate effectively, meaning creativity, problem-solving and critical-thinking abilities are all affected. Finally, eat well. Omega 3, found in fish, soya beans and many seeds, is good for your brain's health. Also eat less saturated fat, found in red meat and dairy products, as it affects your ability to focus and remember.

c *Time management*

Trying to work harder can be demotivating so try the opposite approach. Only go to work for five hours, if you can, and then relax for the rest of the day. When the day is long, tasks can expand to fill the time, you check personal emails more, chat more and surf the web more. By limiting your time, you don't allow so much time for other activities. Gradually increase your working time back up and you'll probably manage to keep doing tasks quicker than before and as a result achieve more.

④ Tell a partner which things in the text you have tried and which you would like to try.

Listening

5))) 7.3 GloCo have organised some more events for the week. Listen and complete Fehim's diary with the events he's going to go to.

MONDAY	2.00–3.00	Team meeting
	3.00–5.00	Project update meeting
TUESDAY	2.00–3.00	*Customer meeting*
	3.00–5.00	*meeting with Simon*
WEDNESDAY	9:00–10:00	Memory and concentration session
	11:00–4:00	Staff training
THURSDAY	9.00–11.00	IT meeting
	1.00–2.00	*lunch with Diane*
	3.00–4.00	Customer meeting
FRIDAY	9.00–12.00	Report writing
	2.00–4.00	Customer meeting

6 Listen again and complete the sentences.

1 I'm *meeting* a customer at 2.00.
2 I'm *working* with Simon on a new project from 3.00 to 5.00.
3 It *starts* at 9.00 on Wednesday.
4 No, I'm *having* lunch with Diane at 1.00. We *going to* out for a pizza.
5 Well, I would go to the session on relaxation, but it *finishes* too late for me.

Grammar

More practice

Future plans, intentions and schedules

Present simple
Use the present simple for schedules or timetabled events in the future.
Often we cannot affect the time these events happen.

It starts at 9.00 on Wednesday.

Present continuous and *be going to*
For intentions and plans, use either *be going to* or the present continuous with no difference in meaning. We are more likely to use present continuous for arrangements.

I'm meeting a customer at 2.00.
I'm going to meet a customer at 2.00.

>>> GRAMMAR REFERENCE PAGE 110

7 Put the verbs in brackets into the correct form of the present simple or continuous.

1 The training session *starts* (start) at 9.00 a.m.
2 I'm *meeting* (meet) Fehim for a coffee at lunchtime.
3 My flight *leaves* (leave) at 8.45.
4 Halide's *working* (work) this Saturday in the office.
5 His train *arrives* (arrive) at 5.00 tomorrow evening.
6 I'm *playing* (play) tennis with my boss later.
7 I'm *going* (go) to Paris at the weekend.
8 She's not available – she *'s seeing* (see) Paula at 12.

Vocabulary

8 Complete the sentences using the words in the box.

| complete | divide | enhance | focus | limit | prioritise | relax |
| remember | set deadlines | take pressure off | | | | |

1 It's important to *set deadlines* that you can meet to avoid stress.
2 Working in a team or being able to delegate can *take pressure off* you.
3 People use a wide range of techniques to *enhance* their performance.
4 I try to *complete* everything on my to-do list by the end of every day.
5 I *divide* my tasks into two lists – things for now and things for the future.
6 I find it difficult to *prioritise* I tend to do the easy things first, not the most important things.
7 I *focus* best in the morning so I do the most difficult jobs then.
8 I *limit* my email use to one hour a day maximum.
9 When I'm stressed, I try to *relax* by going for a walk.
10 I use email reminders to help me *remember* where and when I need to go.

Speaking

9 Work with a partner and discuss the questions.

1 What do you have scheduled regularly in your working week? When and where do these things happen?
2 What plans and intentions do you have this week?
3 How will you make sure you complete all of these events efficiently?

Start up

1))) **7.4 Listen to different people describing the things they hate most about email. Complete the sentences.**

1 1 I hate how _many_ emails I get. I think I can
   just _delete_ ninety per cent of the emails I get.
5 2 I hate how _hard it's to focus_ again after getting an email.
7 3 I hate how I can't _get away from_ email.
2 4 I can't stand _poor subject lines_ or people not
   updating them.
3 5 It really annoys me when people can't _get to the point_
4 6 It drives me crazy when people put _important_
   and it's not.
6 7 It really irritates me when people don't _check for mistakes_

2 Choose the five things in ❶ that annoy you the most. Work with a partner and write five suggestions for good email practice.

People should limit the number of emails they send.

Writing

3 Write the phrases 1–8 in the correct column for where you would use them in an email.

Greeting	First line	Closing line	Sign-off
Hi Halide,	I am writing with reference to …	Hope this helps.	Kind regards
1 Dear Halide 5 Halide	3 thanks for your email 7	4 8	2 cheers 6

F 1 Dear Halide,
I 2 Cheers
N 3 Thanks for your email.
F 4 If you require any further assistance, please
   do not hesitate to contact me.
I 5 Halide
F 6 Yours sincerely
N 7 Got your message, thanks.
N 8 Get back to me if you need anything.

4 Work with a partner. Decide if the phrases from ❸ are formal or informal/neutral.

5 Use phrases from ❸ to complete the emails.

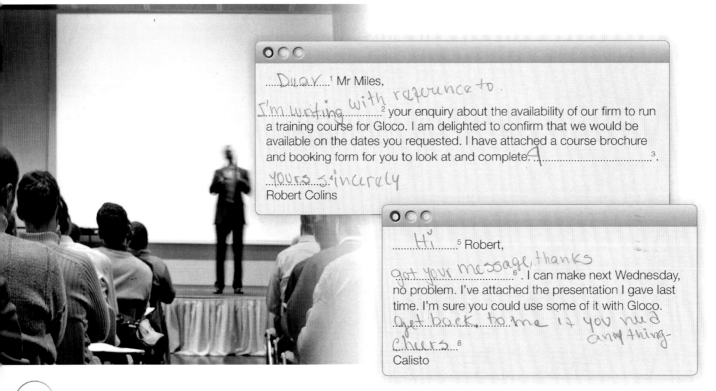

○ ○ ○

Dear [1] Mr Miles,
I'm writing with reference to [2] your enquiry about the availability of our firm to run a training course for Gloco. I am delighted to confirm that we would be available on the dates you requested. I have attached a course brochure and booking form for you to look at and complete. _____ [3].
Yours sincerely [4]
Robert Colins

○ ○ ○

_Hi_ [5] Robert,
Got your message, thanks [6]. I can make next Wednesday, no problem. I've attached the presentation I gave last time. I'm sure you could use some of it with Gloco.
Get back to me if you need anything. [7]
Cheers [8]
Calisto

6 Look at the expressions for making arrangements. Decide if they are formal or informal/neutral.

F 1 I wondered if you had time to …
U 2 Have you got a couple of minutes to …
F 3 I would like to discuss …
I 4 I need to chat about …
F 5 I suggest we meet to discuss things further.
I 6 Whatever's best for you.

7 Use the phrases from **3** and **6** to write two emails.

Email 1 – From Mr Miles to Robert Colins arranging to meet to talk further about their needs for the course.

Email 2 – From Robert to Calisto to arrange to meet to talk about the presentation and course for Gloco.

8 Read the email Calisto sent to a customer the last time he delivered the course. Each sentence is missing one word. Try to correct Calisto's mistakes.

○ ○ ○

Dear Fiona,
I wondered you had time to take a quick look through the course outline? I thought I'd send you a copy the presentation I am planning to give to your staff. It might be a good idea check that this is what you would like. It is only first draft so I will make changes anyway. However, I thought you might like provide some input since this is such a valuable course.
It was a pleasure meeting you last week and I look forward hearing from you soon.
Kind regards
Calisto

9 Work with a partner and look at one of the emails they wrote in **7**. Proofread the email for them. Use the checklist:

- Look out for typical word mistakes, e.g. *there*, *their* and *they're* – your spell checker won't notice them.
- Check for common grammar errors – subject-verb agreement, tense errors, countable and uncountable nouns.
- Check the style is appropriately formal – including the start and finish. If you're not sure, go for a neutral style.
- Check you have referred to (and attached) your attachments.
- Check the subject line is appropriate.

1 Look at the map and discuss the questions with a partner.

1 Which countries might have problems working together because of the time zones? *podrie*

2 How do you think companies deal with such issues?

↓ ↓ ↓inconvenient
lidiar taks

a lo largo de

2 Kaso is a German insurance company that operates throughout Europe. Read the latest company email notice and complete Karl's email to Sofia about the announcements.

Dear all,
We are <u>delighted</u> to announce that Kaso has just bought LPM, a small but competitive insurance firm in the Middle East. LPM's headquarters are in the UAE, but the firm has offices throughout the Middle East. In addition, LPM is at an exciting stage as the firm is growing in Malaysia. These are exciting times for Kaso and for many of our staff with opportunities to live and work internationally.
We are going to form a number of teams to work on a variety of projects. If you are keen to work on this project and help the company move forward, please contact your line manager.
Kind regards,
Didier Remy

Hi Sofia,
Have you seen the news about Kaso buying ....LPM......[1] in ..U.A.E.......[2]? We need to talk about who we can put forward to work from our department. LPM's going to work in Malaysia[3] and there'll be exciting opportunities. Let me know when you can meet.
Best wishes
Karl

3))) 7.5 Listen to Karl and Sofia in Germany discussing the logistics of a team working across the three countries. Complete the table.

	UAE	Malaysia	Germany
Time difference with Germany	+2 hours ahead	+7 hours ahead	☆
Weekend days	Friday and Saturday	Thursday and Friday	Saturday and Sunday

4 With a partner, suggest a plan of when and how they could work together with the time difference problems. Think about:

- when people are all at work.
- how to deal with the different days off.
- how to deal with the different working hours.
- different deadlines that will need to be set for each area.

5 Read the email and complete the to-do list.

○ ○ ○

Dear Scott, Ahad and Svetlana,
We're delighted you have all agreed to work on this project together. I think we all agree this is an exciting time for the company. At this stage, the priority should be for you to formulate a schedule together. We need to set clear goals and you're going to need to plan your working methods. The time differences and working week will not make this easy but could you set up a conference call to discuss this?
Kind regards
Karl and Sofia

To do
Prioritise Formulation schedule togo ther
Set clear goals
Plan working methods

6 Read the emails and discuss the questions with a partner.

1 What problem does Scott have?
2 What's your opinion on the style of Scott's email?

○ ○ ○

Dear Scott and Svetlana,
It's a pleasure to be working with you on this project. May I suggest we arrange a conference call for next Monday at 8.00 a.m. German time?
Kind regards
Ahad

○ ○ ○

Dear Ahad and Scott,
I apologise for not having replied sooner. 8.00 a.m. German time would be absolutely fine for me. I look forward to speaking to you both shortly.
Best regards
Svetlana

○ ○ ○

Guys,
Sorry. No can do. There's no way I'm going to be at work for 8.00 a.m. on a Monday. You'll have to come up with a better idea than that.
Scott

7 Work with a partner and change Scott's email to make it more formal and polite.

8 ◀)) 7.6 Karl sees Scott's email just before he's about to send it. Listen to the changes he suggests and compare it with your own changes.

9 Discuss with a partner what difficulties they might have. Suggest best working practices for:

- when they should send emails.
- when they should make conference calls.
- when they should set deadlines for.

10 ◀)) 7.7 Listen to their call. What three important working practices do they put in place?

1 Deadlines on Tuesday on Wednesday 2 No emails on F and S 3 ....

11 After a few weeks, Svetlana keeps missing conference calls and responding to emails too slowly. She doesn't seem to pay any attention to time differences or how it impacts on other people's working hours. Write an email to Svetlana politely suggesting how the group should work together.

Start up

1 Look at the pictures and discuss with a partner what they're negotiating in each picture.

2 Discuss the questions with a partner.

1 Have you ever negotiated in any of the situations in **1**?
2 How comfortable do you feel negotiating?
3 Do you often try to get a good deal?
4 When was the last time you got a good deal?

Reading

3 Look at the pictures and read about the unusual bonuses offered below. Imagine you can have two of them in your company. Tell a partner which two you would choose and why.

1 Google offers eyebrow shaping at a substantial discount.
2 Employees at an engineering company get $80 as an educational allowance every month.
3 GoDaddy pay part of the costs for employee activities such as whitewater rafting, competitive cooking courses, gold panning, and trapeze classes.
4 FactSet Research offers their workers free lunches, barbecues in the summertime, ice cream get togethers and visits from various local food suppliers.
5 Zappos.com gives a $50 monthly allowance to every employee to award one of their colleagues with a bonus.

4 Decide which company in **3** the sentences are about.

a If you work here, it's important that people like you. .....
b This only helps if you worry about your image. .....
c If you're not careful, you'll put on weight. .....
d If you want to leave the company, this will help you. ..... ,
e If you're adventurous, you'll like working here. .....

Listening

5))) 8.1 Listen to a sports star's contract negotiations. What terms is he negotiating?

1 ....

2 ....

6))) 8.2 Listen to a sports star's agent in contract negotiations. What terms is he negotiating?

1 ....

2 ....

7 Listen to the negotiations again and complete the sentences.

1 If I .... here, I'll need to buy a new house.

2 If the club .... me buy it, I'll be really happy.

3 If you want, the club .... you the money.

4 If you buy me, you .... my image.

5 He .... well if we provide language lessons and a translator to help.

6 If we pay for these, ... he sign the deal?

Grammar

> **Zero and first conditional**
>
> Use the zero conditional sentences to talk about something that is true at any time. It's formed with *if* + present simple + present simple.
>
> If you buy me, you buy my image.
>
> Use the first conditional for a possible condition and a probable result in the future. *If* can be replaced with *when* to show more certainty.
>
> If I move here, I'll need to buy a new house.
> If you want, the club will lend you the money.
>
> It's formed with *if* + present simple + *will*.
> The clauses can come in either order with no change in meaning.
>
> If we provide language lessons, he'll adapt well.
> He'll adapt well if we provide language lessons.

》》GRAMMAR REFERENCE PAGE 110

8 For each situation, write a sentence using the zero or first conditional to explain what will happen.

1 leave the company = have to give a month's notice
   If I want to leave the company, I have to give a month's notice.

2 agree terms = get contract
   ....

More practice

3 pay the whole loan = own the car
   ....

4 break the law = need a lawyer
   ....

5 get more money = move to Madrid (a job you want to take)
   ....

6 be paid overtime = work the hours the boss tells you
   ....

Speaking

9 Work with a partner. Student A, look below. Student B, look at page 98.

You're the manager of a department and are negotiating a contract with a new employee. Your new employee wants to negotiate salary, holiday and hours of work

Salary: From $100,000 to $150,000, but really you would like to pay only $120,000.

Holiday: The standard number of days is 26 and there is no negotiation.

Hours of work: You allow working from home, but normally a maximum of two days per week. Normal hours are 9.00 to 5.00, but you will allow some flexibility between 8.00–10.00 start and 4.00–6.00 finish.

Start up ① Look at the pictures and discuss with a partner which ones are most important for you at work.

| bonuses | health benefits | holidays | pension | salary |

② Tell your partner which one(s) you would change about your current job if you could.

Reading ③ Look at the title and discuss the question with a partner.

WHAT WOULD YOU DO IF YOU COULD NAME YOUR OWN SALARY?

Picture yourself in the final stages of your job interview. The only thing left to talk about is the salary. To your surprise, the interviewer says, 'It's our policy here to let me know what you'd like to make, and we'll finalise the offer.'

So here's the dream scenario. 'I'd like to make $1 million a year!', you shake hands, dance out of the room, and live happily ever after. Easy. But hold on one moment. What if it's not a dream and could be a reality?

1 You still need to perform
Let's say you're a new salesperson at a small company, and for you, a dream salary is $75,000. If your efforts only generated $40,000 in sales, the company would fire you.

2 Everything is relative
If you had a salary of $5 or $10 million, would you be happy? Few people would say no. But what if you were a Hollywood actor? What would you ask for?

3 Do your homework
The most important thing is to know the value of your skills. If you were going to be a senior manager in charge of ten employees, what would you ask for? The simple answer is, if you wanted to get a job offer, you would have to ask for a reasonable salary.

4 Entrepreneurs
Let's say you have your own business which makes $200,000 per year. If you were the boss, would you take $150,000? $175,000? Or is it better to take a salary of $50,000, hire two employees, and expand your company?

5 The workplace is changing
Some companies have dropped their vacation policies in the same way, so that employees can also choose how much holiday they take. This presents a similar dilemma. If you could take any amount of holiday per year, how many days would you take? If you could negotiate all of the conditions of our job – salary, health benefits, vacation, bonuses, and pension – what would be the most important thing for you?

4 Read the text again and answer the questions.

1 What would happen if you made the company less money than your salary?
2 Who would say no if they were offered $5 million?
3 What should you ask for if you were to be the manager of ten employees?
4 What two options does the text give entrepreneurs?
5 What other dilemmas do people face?

Grammar

Second conditional

Use the second conditional to express an unreal or imaginary situation and its possible result. It's unlikely to happen.
It's formed with *if* + past simple + *would*.

If you wanted to get an offer, you'd have to ask for a reasonable salary.
The company would fire you if your efforts only generated $40,000 in sales.
If you were going to be a senior manager in charge of ten employees, what would you ask for?

>>>GRAMMAR REFERENCE PAGE 111

5 Make sentences using the second conditional.

1 have to share an office = quit
   if I had to share my office, I'd quit.

2 boss leaves = apply for his/her job
   ....

3 get a pay rise = go out for dinner
   ....

4 easier job = get a new computer
   ....

5 not be happy = change my job
   ....

6 no free lunch = no staff at meeting
   ....

?

You can use *were* after I/he/she/it in second conditional sentences:
If I were you, I'd sign the contract.
He wouldn't work so hard if he weren't paid a big bonus each year.

More practice

6 Look at the statements. Who thinks they're more likely to get the job?

If I got the job, I'd be happy.

If I hit my targets, the money would be good.

If the money was right, I'd take it.

If I don't get it, I'll be sad.

If the money's right, I will take it.

The money's good if you hit your targets.

Speaking

7 Work with a partner and discuss the questions.

What would you do if …

* you could ask for any salary you wanted?
* you could have more holiday, but had to take a lower salary?
* you were offered a higher salary, but it was commission based?
* you had your own company – pay yourself a higher salary or invest in the company?

Start up

1 Look at the different negotiating situations. Discuss the questions below with a partner.

javivra

vorely

early

- leaving work early
- getting a pay rise
- buying a product in a shop
- making a deal at work (supplier/purchaser)

1 Which situations have you had experience of negotiating in?
2 Do you feel comfortable negotiating? Why/Why not?
3 Some cultures negotiate or bargain in many situations. What situations are common in your culture?
4 Do you think you're good at negotiating? Why/Why not?

Reading

2 Which of the statements 1–4 do you agree with?

1 The price of everything is flexible.
2 I expect 30% discount on any purchase.
3 I try to get a discount when I buy lots of items.
4 If I say the price is too high, I then expect a discount.

3 Read the text and find out which statements in **2** would be true when negotiating in India.

Negotiating in India

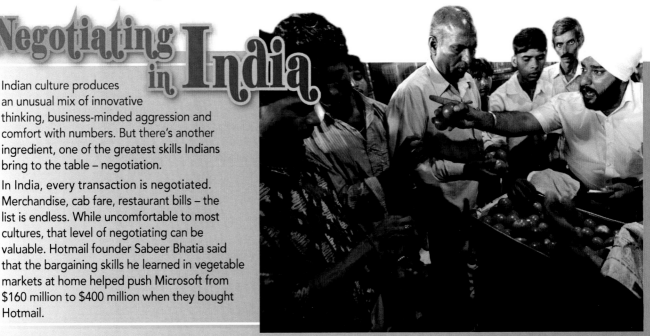

Indian culture produces an unusual mix of innovative thinking, business-minded aggression and comfort with numbers. But there's another ingredient, one of the greatest skills Indians bring to the table – negotiation.

In India, every transaction is negotiated. Merchandise, cab fare, restaurant bills – the list is endless. While uncomfortable to most cultures, that level of negotiating can be valuable. Hotmail founder Sabeer Bhatia said that the bargaining skills he learned in vegetable markets at home helped push Microsoft from $160 million to $400 million when they bought Hotmail.

Here are a few rules for bargaining as a customer in India.

Rule #1 – Price is flexible. There are no suggested retail prices in India. Nothing is labelled, so talk to several sellers before making a major purchase.

Rule #2 – Try for 70% off. Don't accept less than 30%.

Rule #3 – Negotiate one item at a time. If you plan to buy a couple of things, DON'T say so at the start. Get the seller to give you prices on each item to use as a negotiation tool.

Rule #4 – Wait for the pad of paper. When the bargaining gets serious, the pencil and paper come out. Remember the price written down is only the starting point – don't forget rule #2.

Rule #5 – Say 'TOO HIGH', a lot. Don't even begin negotiating until the salesman has lowered the starting price at least twice.

Rule #6 – Imply a bundled purchase. Ask the salesperson what deal they would give you if you bought two items. Add a third item and then add a very expensive fourth item – one which you don't intend to buy. This will excite the salesperson and the price will come down for everything. Lock those prices and drop the expensive item. At this point, you should have saved close to 50%.

Is it a stereotype that Indians are good at negotiating? Sure. Is it accurate? There's only one way to find out.

4 Discuss the questions with a partner.

1 How similar is your culture to India on negotiating?
2 Do you see this style of negotiating as normal or aggressive? Why?
3 If someone negotiated like this in your country, would it work?
4 What would you say are your country's strengths in business?

Listening

5 •))) **8.3** Listen to a price negotiation. Why does it fail?

6 •))) **8.4** Listen to a salary negotiation. Why does it fail?

7 Listen to the two negotiations again and complete the phrases.

1 What I _propose_ is … .
2 What do you have in _mind_ ?
3 Let me just check I _understand_ you correctly.
4 Would you be willing to accept a _compromise_ ?
5 That would be _difficult_ for us.
6 At the moment, we don't see this as a _viable_ option.
7 One _option_ would be to …
8 If I understand you _correctly_.
9 What if we offered you an _alternative_ ?
10 I'm afraid we could only accept this on one _condition_

8 Write the phrases from **7** in the correct place in the table.

a reaching a deal	b bargaining	c rejecting
We seem to be nearing agreement. That sounds like a deal.	10 9	5 6

d putting forward a proposal	e clarifying	f exploring positions
7 1	3 8 2	4

9 Put the stages a–f in **8** in order from the start to the end of a negotiation.

Speaking

10 Work with a partner and hold four negotiations using the flow chart below.

* swap desks with your partner
* buy your partner's car
* ask your partner to complete some of your work
* decide who pays for lunch

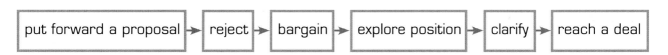

put forward a proposal → reject → bargain → explore position → clarify → reach a deal

11 Work with another pair. Take turns to listen to each other negotiate. While you listen, tick (✓) the phrases each pair uses from **8**. Also monitor for politeness and give feedback.

Scenario: A tough deal

1 ·))) **8.5** You have been put in charge of sourcing new company cars and negotiating a good price. Listen to the opinions of three key people and complete the information.

Sales manager	Senior management executive	Car pool manager
His team needs _10_ [1] cars.	Senior management needs _6_ [6] cars.	The company needs _10_ [1] pool cars.
They're used for _sales_ [2].	They're used for _getting to and from work_ [7].	They're used for _customer visits_ [?], travel and training
The most important features are • _good boot space_ • _Bluetooth_ • _inbuilt satnav_ _Inbuilt Satellite Navigation_	The most important features are • _cruise control_ • _good interior_ • _good fuel economy_	The most important features are • _efficient & cheap to run_ • _low insurance and service cost_ • _adjustable seats_

2 Read the information from the online car guide and answer the questions.

1 According to the car guide, which is the best car?
2 Which car has the fewest additional features available?
3 Which car has the most of these features available?
4 Which one is the most fuel efficient?

Car Guide The best choice of cars

	Skoda Citigo Hatchback 1.0 60 S 5dr	Kia Optima Saloon 1.7 CRDi 1 4dr	Toyota Prius Hatchback 1.8 VVT-i T Spirit 5dr
Price	£7,980	£19,595	£24,910
Verdict	5 out of 5 stars	2 out of 5 stars	3 out of 5 stars
Air conditioning	Not available	Standard	Not available
Cruise control	Not available	Standard	Standard
Heated seats	Not available	Not available	Pack only
MP3 connection	Standard	Standard	Standard
Satellite navigation	Pack only	Not available	Standard
Leather seats	Not available	Not available	£1,500
Bluetooth	Pack only	Standard	Standard
Average mpg*	101	92.7	113.6
Typical insurance	£273	£522	£501
Three-year servicing	£457	£768	£682
Boot space	251–951 litres	505 litres	445 litres

* Miles per gallon

pack only – can be added at an additional cost

3 Discuss with a partner which car you think would be best for each group.

4 You've contacted the car sales company to get an initial quote. Read the email and answer the questions.

1 What range of discounts can be offered? *5% to 15%*
2 What's the range of prices quoted? *£164,000 to 510,000*
3 What else is negotiable?

○ ○ ○

Dear Sir/Madam,

Thank you for your enquiry reagrading the quote for your company's new cars.

With the purchase of 26 cars, we could only offer a discount of 5% if a minimum of eight of each model were purchased. However, we could offer a discount of 10% if twelve of two different models were bought and a 15% discount if only one model was bought.

It will obviously depend on your company's needs and budget and at the moment the packages I could offer you range from £164,000 to £510,000. The additional features in each car are also negotiable.

I look forward to meeting you tomorrow to discuss the deal in more detail.

Best wishes

Mark

---

5 Work with a partner. You have to report back to the manager on the different options and together decide on the best deal. Make a note of the options you're presented with. Try to use expressions with *if*:

If we buy the Toyota Prius, it will be the most economical car.
We could buy a more energy-efficient car if we had a bigger budget.
If we want satellite navigation, the Kia isn't an option.

6 Student A, you're going to try to negotiate the best deal for your company. Read the details agreed with your manager below. Student B, you're the car salesperson. Look at your information on page 98.

> You have a total of £365,000 to spend.
> You want to buy 14 Skoda Citigos and 12 Toyota Prius.
> You want 15% discount.
> You want free insurance on all cars.
> You want free seat height adjustment, Bluetooth and satellite navigation in the Skodas.
> Try to reach a deal on the servicing to keep in budget.

Start up

1 Look at the pictures of some common mistakes people can make at work. Work with a partner and try to add other ideas.

Where on earth is it?

I can't believe I just sent that to my boss.

Hmm. I wonder what's in here.

I'm really sorry I missed that deadline.

2 Discuss the questions with a partner.

1 How do you feel when people you work with make the kind of mistakes in **1**?

2 How do you feel when you make these kinds of mistakes?

3 Do you think it's important to find out whose fault something was? Give reasons for your answer.

blame – to think or say that someone's responsible for something bad that has happened or gone wrong

fault – responsibility for a mistake or bad situation

responsibility – a duty to deal with something so that it's your fault if something goes wrong

Reading

3 Read the texts about different mistakes people made. Match each text with a situation in the box.

a presentation   a production line   a sales visit

1 Laura Ossana

When I left the office to go on my last sales call, I couldn't find where I had put the map showing me how to find the customer's office. I didn't have enough time to print a new one, but I was quite confident I could find my way. I remembered from a previous visit that it was only five minutes from the train station, but I had thought it was easier than it was and in the end I couldn't find it.

2 Vera Millers

We had an important deadline to meet when the machines stopped working the other day. I wasn't worried because I knew how long it would take and that we had plenty of time to fix it, but I had worked out the time wrongly and we got to the end of the time available to meet the order.

3 Giorgios Varnava

I didn't remember that I had to give a talk in a team meeting until I looked at my calendar that morning. I had a couple of hours to prepare, but I was under so much pressure I wrote some of the figures incorrectly. This caused a lot of confusion and, of course, I wasn't ready for all the questions that were asked. It was a disaster!

4 Read the texts again and replace the highlighted phrases with the correct forms of the verbs in the box.

be unprepared	break down	forget	get lost	mislay
miscalculate	mistype	run out of	underestimate (it)	

Listening

5 You're going to listen to Laura, Vera and Giorgios describing other mistakes that were made on their projects. Before you listen, complete the sentences with the correct form of some of the words from **4**.

1 Even though I had planned exactly what I wanted to say, I ...forgot... so many things.
2 I think they thought I was really ...unprepared... and not very professional.
3 When I did, I realised I had ...mislaid... their contact details.
4 Unfortunately, I ...mistyped... their email address and sent it to the wrong person.
5 I hadn't .... ; I had simply mistyped.
miscalculate.

6 ◁)) 9.1 Listen and check your answers.

Grammar

> **Past perfect**
>
> Use the past perfect to talk about an action in the past that was completed before another action in the past.
>
> I couldn't find where I **had put** the map.
> put the map somewhere → couldn't find it
> I realised I **had forgotten** their contact details.
> forgot their details → realised the mistake

⟩⟩⟩GRAMMAR REFERENCE PAGE 112

More practice

7 Match the statements 1–6 with the responses a–f.

1 Were you surprised when they didn't call? d
2 Why didn't you use the satnav on your phone? a
3 Had you worked with the client before? c
4 The presentation was quickly becoming a disaster because my figures were wrong. e
5 The food was bad and the client had to pay. b
6 The hotel was awful! f

a I had forgotten it. I couldn't even phone the client to say I was going to be late.
b Why? Had you lost your wallet?
c We hadn't done much business but we knew each other's work well.
d I knew them well so it was fine.
e Once I identified what had happened, it was easy to explain.
f Hadn't you stayed there before?

8 Use the prompts to write sentences explaining what went wrong.

	Result	Reason
1	late for work	lost key
2	got lost	satnav battery went flat
3	lost money	underestimated the costs
4	missed flight	car broke down

I was late for work because I had lost my key.

Speaking

9 Write down some mistakes you've made.

10 Ask your partner questions to find out more about their mistake and how it was resolved.

Start up Look at the situations and discuss the questions with a partner.

1 Do you have insurance for any of these things? What other things do you have insurance for?
2 Would you make an insurance claim in each of these cases?
3 Do you think more or fewer people make insurance claims in your country now compared to the past?

?

insurance – regularly paying a company money so that they will give you money if something you own is damaged, lost or stolen, or if you die, or are ill or injured

compensation – money that someone receives because something bad has happened to them

Reading **2** Read the text and decide which statement best matches the author's opinion.

1 People don't need insurance; they just need to be more careful.
2 People need more insurance to protect them.
3 People don't try to blame other people very often.

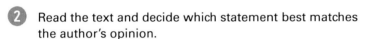

In some countries, such as Britain and the USA, a 'compensation culture' has developed. In one situation, someone was holding a hot cup of coffee when a person bumped into them. Whose fault was it? If the person had sat down and drunk the coffee, it wouldn't have happened. Was it the other person's fault? They weren't looking where they were going. Was it the coffee company's fault? They had made the coffee too hot.

Think of some of the labels on products. Most irons contain the warning 'do not iron clothes whilst wearing them'. Companies have had to place the warning there to protect themselves from more people making a claim. Should the company really be blamed? One person was wearing the clothes when they used the iron. At what point do we stop blaming the iron and start blaming the person?

Companies are clearly protecting themselves more and more. Perhaps the way forward is, as in many other countries, for everyone to protect themselves with insurance. The next time a person spills coffee on a carpet, the insurance can pay and not the friend. In some countries, this would be the norm, but in other countries this would be a big change in the culture, but perhaps a better one than the current compensation culture. At least the insurance companies will be happy with all the extra work.

3 Read the text again. Are the sentences true or false?

1 Attitudes to compensation have changed in the UK.
2 Someone has probably ironed their clothes whilst wearing them.
3 The author thinks the company that makes a product is always to blame.
4 The author thinks that it can be a good idea to let insurance companies deal with accidents.
5 All countries would find it normal to make an insurance claim for an accident.

Listening

4 •))) 9.2 Listen to three people describing accidents. Tick (✓) what went wrong in each situation.

1   a   a car hit her ☐   b   she hit a car ☐

2   a   he hurt his leg ☐   b   he hurt his back ☐

3   a   she spilt a drink on her phone ☐   b   she spilt a drink on her computer ☐

5 Listen again. What were they doing when the accident happened?

1   2   3   ....

Grammar

Past simple, past continuous, past perfect
Form the past continuous with *was/were* + verb + *-ing*
a Unfinished or interrupted actions in the past. Used with the past simple.
I was driving to work when I had an accident.
b Actions around a particular time in the past.
I was speaking on the phone all morning on a conference call.
c When an action is completed, use the past simple.
I knocked it all over my computer.
Form the past perfect with *had* + the past participle.
d Use the past perfect when one action happens before another.
I had had a bad back for a week, but fell and hurt my leg as well.

》》GRAMMAR REFERENCE PAGE 111

More practice

6 Complete the text with the correct form of the verbs in brackets.

For centuries, the people of Bhutan ~~were~~ *lived/living* ¹ (live) a rural and quite basic life. Even until the late 1990s, people ~~had/had not~~ *didn't have* ² (not/have) televisions. However, in 1998 thousands of people *were watching* ³ (watch) the 1998 World Cup final while they *were standing* ⁴ (stand) in the main square. It was so popular that the king *had decided* ⁵ (decide) to allow television into his country. Until then the king ....⁶ (ban) TV, and he ....⁷ (not/allow) advertising either. In 1999, the king ....⁸ (allow) TVs into the country for the first time. As people ....⁹ (start) to watch a lot of television, children ....¹⁰ (fight) more, crime ....¹¹ (increase) and families ....¹² (break up).

Speaking

7 Work with a partner. Look at the pictures and describe what you think has happened.

8 Imagine you have to complete an accident record at work. Write sentences using the past simple, past continuous and past perfect describing what happened in these pictures.

Start up

1 Tell a partner what you think each person might be apologising for in the pictures.

2 Discuss with a partner how you would feel in each situation.

A colleague …
- makes a mistake but doesn't apologise.
- apologises a lot but keeps making the same mistakes.
- only apologises if someone notices they have made a mistake.

Reading

3 What do you think are the most important things to do when you realise you've made a mistake? Write down your ideas, then read the text and compare with the text.

Risky business

Risk communications consultant, Peter Sandman, has a lot of experience in helping clients who are in a difficult situation. He believes an apology can help when mistakes have been made, but feels people don't always know how to apologise or how important it can be. He suggests taking the following steps:

1 Say what you did. Don't be vague. Just a clear and brief statement: 'This is what we did wrong'. Then, in a few words, explain the reason why you did what you did and do not mention things outside your control too much – it looks like you want an excuse.

2 Say you're sorry. Make your apology as heartfelt as you can without taking the blame: 'I regret what happened to you' is too impersonal. 'I feel terrible about what I did' is good. 'It's entirely my fault' is dangerous.

3 Make it right. Do your best to correct the problem. Making it right doesn't have to mean making it perfect but your intention has to be genuine and the progress you make in rectifying the situation real. However, promising more than you can deliver is a sure way to disappoint if you fail to keep your promise.

4 Get the timing right. One act of showing a client that you're sorry can be to provide compensation. If you offer compensation too soon, however, the 'victim' may think that it's a substitute for saying you're sorry. People want to see that a problem has been corrected before receiving any form of compensation.

5 Show that you've learned your lesson. Demonstrate that you're sorry. Show an act of kindness to the person you're apologising to. Without this, the process of apologising won't be complete.

4 Read the text again and answer the questions.

1 How should you deliver your apology?
2 Why should you not discuss things outside your control too much?
3 Should you take all the blame?
4 Why shouldn't you make too many promises for the future?
5 What does Peter Sandman say about compensation?

Listening

5 ·))) 9.3 Listen to four conversations and number the situations.

☐ 3 The person has bought the wrong thing.　☐ 4 The person has been given the wrong food.
☐ 1 The phone call gets cut off.　☐ 2 Someone has been sent the wrong order.

6 Listen again and complete the sentences.

1 Sorry about ....*that*.... . I'm not sure what happened.
2 Don't ....*worry*.... about it.
3 It ...*must*... ...*have*... been mixed up with another order.
4 Please ....*accept*.... our apologies.
5 I ....*hope*.... it hasn't caused too much inconvenience.

6 I'm ...*afraid*... I bought the wrong size.
7 No ....*problem*.... . We can just replace it.
8 I think it must ....*have*.... ....*been*.... on the wrong hanger.
9 Sorry, I ..*'ll*.. take it back.
10 There ....*'ll*.... be no charge for your meal.

7 Write the phrases in **6** in the correct column.

Apologising	Responding to an apology	Giving an explanation	Showing concern	Offering to put things right
4	2	3	1	7
5	6	8	9	10

Say it right

8 How do you think the intonation of the word *sorry* is different in each of the situations? Discuss your ideas with a partner.

9 ·))) 9.4 Listen and check.

Speaking

10 Work with a partner and role play the situations using phrases from **6**.

Student A	Student B
You serve a nice steak for dinner when your guest reminds you that they're vegetarian. Apologise for the situation.	
	Respond to the apology.
Give an explanation and offer to put things right.	
	An important customer phones and their order is late. Apologise for the situation.
Respond to the apology.	
	Give an explanation and offer to put things right.

Scenario: Supply problems

1 Match the drinks 1–6 with their possible uses a–f.

1 cherry juice   2 coffee   3 cola   4 cold tea   5 lemon juice   6 milk

a build muscles   b water houseplants   c clean windows   d clean burnt pans   e wake you up if you're feeling tired   f help you go to sleep

2 Work with a partner and compare your answers.

3 Look at the map. The countries in orange are the top ten producers of one of the products in ①. Discuss with a partner which product you think it is.

MEXICO

GUATEMALA

COLOMBIA

BRAZIL

COTE D'IVOIRE

ETHIOPIA

UGANDA

INDIA

VIETNAM

INDONESIA

4 You work for Alto Café, a succesful chain of cafés, which buys coffee from a supplier called Cote Coffee. Read the cards with a partner and decide what to do.

1 Alto Café places a bulk order of coffee beans via the Cote Coffee website on 29th May, but a month later the order still hasn't arrived.

A Don't worry. Alto Café has enough stock for a month. You decide to wait two more weeks before chasing the order. > Go to 2.

B You decide to phone their head office to check what has happened to the order.
> Go to 3.

2 The delivery arrived, but two types of beans were missing and there was no paperwork with the order.

A Wait to see if they come separately – this happened last time and might happen again. > Go to 4.

B You worry that you only have two weeks' stock left now. Phone the head office and chase the order. > Go to 6.

3 You phoned Cote Coffee's head office, but there was no record of the order. They weren't very helpful.

A You decide to give up on this supplier and place an order with Rift Coffee.
> Go to 5.

B You decide to contact another café owner who uses the same supplier.
> Go to 7.

4 The order turns up five weeks late and you lose too many customers. Your business fails and closes.

5 Your business was growing. Your coffee had been the most popular brand across the city. When you change your beans, people start complaining. You lose so many customers to a rival chain that you have to close your business.

6 Head office track down the order and realise it had been sent to a different firm by accident. They send you a new order which arrives in two weeks. Congratulations — you're still in business.

7 The owner tells you that they have had no problems with Cote Coffee. You decide to wait. The other café actually has your order, but doesn't tell you. Your supply problems mean you lose customers and have to fire staff.

5 Work with a partner and discuss the questions.

1 Read cards 3 and 6 if you haven't already. How did Cote Coffee handle the situation?
2 How might it have been handled more effectively?
3 What changes could they make to improve their service?

6 Work with a partner. Student A, read the card below. Student B, read the card on page 99.

> You work for Alto Café in their purchasing department. After the problems with Cote Coffee, your manager has asked you to regularly chase orders from all suppliers to make sure they arrive on time.
> Your sandwich supplier only sent 15 of each type of sandwich to your main shop instead of 50. Phone ToGo and find out what happened. You're not happy and want a discount.

7 9.5 Listen to a phone call between Alto Café and ToGo and answer the questions.

1 What mistake was made?
2 How does Julia deal with the problem?

8 Work in groups of three. Choose a role below and read the information in your role card carefully. Then discuss the situation in your group and decide:

* who's responsible.
* who should apologise.
* what can be done.

ALTO CAFÉ PURCHASING MANAGER

You have checked your emails and are happy that everything happened correctly from Alto Café's end. You don't care whose fault it was, but you plan to use this as a negotiating position for future deals. If they can't do a deal, you will change supplier. You want a 50% reduction on the cost of orders for the next month or a 30% reduction for three months.

DELIVERY COMPANY MANAGER

You know it was your company's fault, but you are always turning down work because your company is so busy. You don't need to keep the customer, but because you feel some loyalty to ToGo, you will offer a 5% discount over two months.

ToGo SALES MANAGER

The emails show that the delivery company made the mistake. You want the delivery company to offer discounted delivery for the next month, around 10% of the cost of the food. Alto Café are an important client and you don't want to lose them. You can offer a meal deal that will save them another 25%.

Start up

① Work with a partner. Look at the pictures and discuss the most important things to consider when you buy these things. Think about quality, price, who made it, where it's made, etc.

② Tell your partner what environmental issues people think about when they buy these products.

Reading

③ Work in groups of three and choose one text each. Quickly read your text and then tell your group what the main idea is.

Meals-on-wheels

Santropol Roulant is an organisation providing healthy, sustainable meals to Montreal citizens who cannot leave their own home. Instead of relying on cars or vans like traditional Meals-on-Wheels, they deliver on bicycles.

But cutting emissions from their delivery wasn't enough for the organisation. They hired Natural Step (a non-profit research and education group) to help further reduce their environmental impact.

Now they grow fruit and vegetables in organic gardens on top of buildings, and recycle their food waste in basements using worms. The compost is given to urban farmers to support them starting their own gardens.

?

sustainable – able to continue for a long time at the same level. Often linked to not damaging the environment.

emission – a substance such as a gas that goes into the air. Often linked to gases that damage the environment.

organic – produced without chemicals

carpooling – sharing cars with other people

Fix-it

At Amsterdam's first Repair Café people can bring in whatever they want to have repaired, at no cost, by volunteers who just like to fix things. Around 30 Repair Cafés have started across the Netherlands. Neighbours donate their skills and labour for a few hours a month to mend clothing, coffee makers, broken lamps, vacuum cleaners and toasters and much more. Martine Postma, a former journalist, started the idea to stop people throwing away so much. 'The things we throw away are usually not that broken. There are more and more people in the world, and we can't keep handling things the way we do. I had the feeling I wanted to do something, not just write about it.'

The Repair Café Foundation has received enquiries from France, Belgium, Germany, Poland, Ukraine, South Africa and Australia for help starting similar schemes.

9th May 2012 ©The New York Times

Car share

Australian based start-up Jayride helps you get from A to B, suggests car sharing, or carpooling, as well as buses, and other options if there are no carpools available. Since 2008, Jayride has been one of Australia's leading sources of carpooling. Jayride collaborates with music festivals to solve transport problems – 3,000 cars carpooled to Splendour in the Grass festival. They also help tourists see sights in ways that are greener and more fun. To date, they have about 7,000 members who've shared 80,000 rides. Consistent carpoolers save 1.38 tonnes of carbon emissions a year and about $2,400. By helping Australians fill empty seats in cars, buses, trains and ferries, Jayride helps reduce traffic and the nation's need for fuel.

4 Read all of the texts and answer the questions.

1 Where do Santropol Roulant grow some of their food?
2 What do Santropol Roulant do with their waste?
3 How many Repair Cafés are there in the Netherlands?
4 Who started the Repair Café and why?
5 How many members does Jayride have?
6 How much money can people save per year?

Vocabulary

5 Complete the questions with a highlighted word from the text in **3**.

1 Do you try to ..reduce.. your carbon footprint?
2 How do you try to ..recycle.. energy? save
3 Have you ever car ..repaired.. share
4 Do you ..donate.. your skills to help others? donate
5 Do you ..collaborates.. any green charities? support
6 Do you know if your company..collabora.. with any green organisations?
7 Is it common to ..save.. recycle waste in your country?
8 Do you get things ..repair.. or do you throw them away?

More practice

6 Work with a partner and answer the questions in **5**.

Listening

7))) **10.1** Listen to Marcus Dowse talking about a 'go-green' initiative in his company. Tick (✓) the things his company tried.

✓ bike scheme	✓ car pooling	✓ growing vegetables	recycling
reducing printing	✓ turning off appliances		

8 Listen again and answer the questions.

1 What was the percentage reduction in cars on site?
2 How much energy does turning off appliances save?
3 Why didn't the bike scheme work?
4 What's the main benefit of growing vegetables?

Speaking

9 Discuss with a partner which things in **7** would work in your workplace.

Start up

1 Look at the picture of a traditional British meal and discuss the questions with a partner.

1 Could you buy most of these ingredients in your country?
2 How many kilometres do you think the average Sunday lunch travels to get to the dinner plate in Britain?
  a 500   c 20,000
  b 7,000   d 30,000
  Check your answer on page 99.
3 Do you know where the food you buy is produced?

2 Look at the things you have in your pockets and in your bag. Tell your partner where they were made.

3 Discuss with your partner the advantages and disadvantages of buying local products.

Reading

4 Read the article and choose the best title.

  a Italian food   b Made in Italy   c Where to shop in Italy

Gorgonzola

Gorgonzola has reportedly been produced in the town of the same name since 879. Today, it's mainly produced in the northern Italian regions of Piedmont and Lombardy.

Lavazza

The coffee company was started in 1895 in Turin. The goods on sale are produced or processed directly at the shop: soap, spirits, oil, spices and, of course, coffee. The headquarters are still in Turin, but today the coffee's sold in over 90 countries.

Balsamic vinegar

Balsamic vinegar has been made in Modena and Reggio Emilia since the Middle Ages: the production of the balsamic vinegar is mentioned in a document dated 1046. The names 'Aceto Balsamico Tradizionale di Modena' and 'Aceto Balsamico Tradizionale di Reggio Emilia' are protected by the European Union's Protected Designation of Origin.

Gucci

Gucci was established in Florence in 1921. While many Italian brands have separated from their Italian roots, even today Gucci is strongly linked to Italy's Tuscan region. 100% of its leather goods, shoes and ready-to-wear are still produced in its Florence workshops.

Vespa

Vespas were first made in Pontedera. Nearly 140 versions of the Vespa have been made. Vespas haven't always been manufactured only in Italy; they have been manufactured all over the world.

Bread

Italy has many regional breads. In Sardinia, the most popular bread is called 'carasau'. It's thin, round and crisp so that it can be kept and used for long periods.

Ceramics

Caltagirone is known as the 'the city of Sicilian ceramics' due to its 1,000-year-old tradition. They are still popular objects to collect, use or give as a present today and are produced by 150 studios and around 600 people.

5 Read the article again and answer the questions.

1 How many types of Vespa have been manufactured?
2 How long has balsamic vinegar been made for?
3 How many people are employed by the ceramic industry in Caltagirone?
4 Where's Lavazza coffee sold today?
5 Where's Gorgonzola mainly produced today?
6 Can Carasau be kept for a long time?
7 Where's Gucci linked to in Italy?

Say it right

6 Find the words in **bold** below in the text in **4**. How do you think the pronunciation is different in each case?

1 The farm's **produce** is sold at local markets.
2 The ceramics have many different **use**s.
3 Many local products are sold in **separate** shops and not big stores.
4 Some people **object** to so many goods being imported.
5 They **present**ed her with a Gucci bag.

7 ◁))) **10.2** Listen and check. Go to page 127 to see the full audioscript

Grammar

> **Passives**
>
> The passive is formed with different tenses of the verb *be* + the past participle
>
> Today, it**'s** mainly **produced** in the northern Italian regions of Piedmont and Lombardy.
>
> Gucci **was established** in Florence in 1921.
>
> Balsamic vinegar **has been made** in Modena and Reggio Emilia since the Middle Ages.
>
> More and more products **are being given** a protected status.
>
> It's used to focus on when, where or what was done rather than who did it.

〉〉〉GRAMMAR REFERENCE PAGE 112

8 Complete the sentences with the correct form of the passive.

1 Most products in the world today .... (manufacture) in China.
2 The majority of olives .... (grow) in Spain.
3 The first Mercedes-Benz vehicles .... (produce) in 1926. The cars .... (produce) in Germany since then, but today they .... (also / make) in nearly twenty other countries.
4 Most pistachios .... (grow) in Iran, but the majority .... (consume) in China.
5 Coffee came to Mexico at the end of the eighteenth century, but it .... (not / export) in great quantities until the 1870s.
6 Petroleum products .... (use) for centuries. Today, most petroleum .... (drill) for in Saudi Arabia.
7 Many industries in the UK .... (affect) by strong competition from other countries. Today, the economy .... (base) on services.
8 More water per person .... (use) in the UAE than in any other country in the world.

More practice

9 Think about a product from your country and write sentences describing when, where and how it was made.

Speaking

10 Work with a partner and discuss the questions.

1 What products are made in your country? How long have they been made there?
2 What foods are grown in your country? How long have they been grown there?
3 Which regions are famous for different products?
4 Do you buy local or seasonal products?
5 Which cars or bikes are made in your country? Who are they used by?
6 Which fashion brands are made in your country? Who are they bought by?

Start up

1 Look at the pictures with a partner and discuss any trends you know about in each sector.

2 Discuss the questions with a partner.

1 How important is it for each of these industries to keep up with consumer trends?
2 How important is it for your industry to keep up with consumer trends?

Reading

3 Discuss the questions with a partner and then compare your ideas with the text.

1 Which do you think is most important for the majority of people?

| price | products | being natural | quality |

2 Are people prepared to pay more for organic, locally-sourced or fair trade products?
3 Do you think attitudes to 'green' products are the same across the world?

Going green

From beauty products to household goods and groceries, the terms 'green,' 'organic,' 'locally sourced,' and 'fair trade,' have begun to appear on more and more labels and ingredient lists within the last decade, but how important are these concepts? Euromonitor International surveyed in-country analysts and in-house researchers in 80+ countries across the globe to learn more about current local views of 'green' features and how these impact purchasing decisions. Here's what they found.

Green factors do influence many respondents' purchase decisions, but they're behind price and quality by a significant margin. 97% think that the quality of a product is a key feature and 85% feel just as strongly about price.

The term 'natural' is an essential factor to nearly 50% of analysts, making it as important as a strong brand. The survey shows that some other 'green' phrases (organic, locally-sourced, fair-trade) only affect about one third of respondents' purchasing decisions.

Only 27% of analysts actively feel the packaging of a product is significant.

Is the higher price justified?

Nearly 70% of respondents across the globe said they would spend more on a green product. Only 11% of respondents were not willing at all to spend more money for green features.

How the world sees 'green'

In the USA, Canada, Europe, and Africa, among others, respondents said that only wealthy people purchase green products. In North America, 'green' is trendy and no longer seen as a 'hippie' idea. Respondents from Latin America emphasised that it's more important for the younger generation. Respondents from Russia and non-EU countries highlighted the lack of available green products in their regions. Analysts in China recognised the organic trend, but feel it is very much still developing.

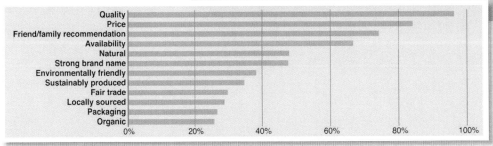

Source: http://blog.euromonitor.com/2012/03/quick-pulse-green-buying-an-exploration-of-green-consumer-trends.html

4 Read the text again. Are the sentences true or false?

1 Very few people are concerned about price.
2 The term *organic* is more important than *natural*.
3 Around one in four people are concerned about packaging.
4 Most people won't pay a higher price for green products.
5 Being green is fashionable in the USA and Canada.
6 Being green is a youth trend in Latin America.
7 Russians buy a lot of green products.
8 People in China are becoming more concerned about green issues.

Listening

5 •)) 10.3 Zlatan works for a large supermarket chain. Listen to his report on a recent customer survey. What do the numbers refer to?

a 180%　　b 24%　　c $500m　　d 110

6 Match the beginnings of the phrases 1–8 with the endings a–h.

1 Could you fill us in on	a previous years?
2 According to	b many surveys, the market for green goods is up 180%.
3 How does this compare to	c it's now 24% of our sales.
4 Roughly speaking,	d the details of the survey?
5 Can we look at the figures for	e the sales are worth $500 million.
6 The end result is	f overall sales?
7 The main trend is	g for growth.
8 What's that in terms of	h the growth of our product range?

7 Listen again and check your answers.

8 Write the phrases in **6** in the correct column.

Asking for information	Reporting information

Speaking

9 Work with a partner to discuss further results of the survey. Student A, look at the table below. Student B, look at page 99. Ask and answer questions to complete the table.

	Survey results			Survey comments
Money spent on green food products	1			Most people said they spent more on green products today than five years ago
How often do you buy green food products?	Every day 30%　Every week 40%	Every month 20%　Never 10%		2 ....
Most common green products bought	Coffee 30%　Vegetables 40%	Snacks 10%　Toilet paper 20%		3 ....
Other green lifestyle choices	4			Energy-saving light bulbs are used more than any other energy saving product.
Age of green shoppers	Percentage of shoppers in each age category considered green Under 18　10% 18–25　30% 26–35　40% 36–45　35% 46–55　30% 55+　10%			5 ....

Scenario: Going green

1 Look at the reasons a company might choose to have a green policy. Which ones do you think are most likely and why?

> good for public relations   reduce environmental impact   save money

2 Wayland surveyed its employees to get suggestions for making their company greener. Look below at some of the most common problems and discuss with a partner which ones you think your company could try to resolve.

Problem	Percentage of staff
Too much paper is wasted.	
Too much non-work waste is produced, e.g. food packaging, magazines and drinks cups.	
Not enough waste is recycled.	
The heating's left on for too long.	
Too much energy is lost in the building.	
Lights are left on too frequently.	
Too many people drive to work.	

3 ⬙)) **10.4** Listen to the results of Wayland's survey and complete the table in **2**.

4 Read the schemes Wayland are planning and answer the questions.

1 Which schemes focus on cutting energy use?
2 Which ones will possibly save the company money?
3 Which ones do you think will be good for publicity?
4 Which ones cut waste?
5 Which ones will cost the company money?

Living roof
Growing a garden on our office roof is simple to do and has many environmental benefits. The building is better insulated from heat loss in the winter and heat gain in the summer. Urban pollution is also absorbed. Rainwater run-off is reduced by at least 50%, which helps prevent flooding. The gardens also attract wildlife, particularly birds.

Cycle-to-work week
Cycling can easily be part of your everyday life. It's recommended by the government that people take two and a half hours exercise a week. To help improve the health and well-being of staff and cut our environmental impact, the company's offering free breakfasts every day to all staff who cycle to work next week.

Car share day
There are 500 employees in our office and our car park has recently been expanded to 400 parking spaces. However, arrive at work after 8.30 and there's nowhere to park. For every space that isn't used each day, Wayland will donate $10 to charity.

Food box delivery
Too much packaging is collected in our bins on a daily basis. From next Monday, fruit boxes will be delivered to the company from a local organic supplier. For every piece of fruit that is purchased, employees will be entitled to an additional piece for free.

Cup for life
Over 350,000 paper cups are used every year in this company. From Monday, employees will be given a free cup for life to replace all the paper cups used.

5 Discuss with a partner which suggestions in **4** you think are best and why. Think about:
- the image of the company
- the reaction of staff
- the money saved.

6 The government has started a Go Green initiative and asked local businesses to be involved. Read the information and discuss with a partner which two initiatives in **4** in Wayland should put forward for this competition.

Nearly 700 kg of waste per person is thrown into landfill every year in our city.

Journey times across the city are now as slow as 8 kph average speed at peak times.

25% of all energy use is lost due to inefficient buildings.

As part of Earth Week, the local government would like companies to submit their own schemes into a competition. The event is being covered all week by local television, newspapers and websites. Special attention will be given to companies that show particularly innovative ideas.

7 Work in groups of four. Pair A, look below. Pair B, look at page 100.

You're keen for your workplace to become greener and want to propose the following ideas:
- The heating's currently controlled centrally and you want each room to be able to control its own temperature.
- Most people currently drive to work and you want the company to provide buses from three main areas across the city.
- You want the company to monitor each department's energy use to create a competition to cut energy costs.

Before your meeting, think about the arguments against each idea that the company might give and how you could counter the argument.

Pairwork

Unit 1   page 9

Student B

You want to speak to Margaret Johnson. Your number is 07665 89241.

Unit 2   page 19

Student A

Career path and promotions
80% of staff weren't happy with their chance of promotion.
75% were pleased with their career path so far.

Comments
I was doing the same things last year that I am now. My job just doesn't change any more.
I got promoted three years in a row, now all the top jobs are filled by people from out of the company.

Unit 3   page 26

Student B

THE CASTLE

A 400-year-old castle on the edge of town provides stunning views over the city and the surrounding countryside. The castle is a much loved tourist site and is popular for weddings and corporate events.

We have different sized rooms to meet your needs. For up to 50 guests, the Balmoral room can be hired. For up to 100 guests, the Blenheim room can be used and for larger events the Main Hall can be hired. The cost to hire each room is:

- Balmoral: £300
- Blenheim: £800
- The Main Hall: £1,500

We offer a range of food and drink services with canapés and drinks ranging from £15 to £30 per head. A traditional carvery can be served in the Main Hall or the Blenheim room for £25 per head or a waiter and waitress service can be provided in all rooms for between £30 and £90 per head.

Live music and other events can also be arranged on request.

Unit 3   page 27

Student B

You're very keen on booking the castle. You think it matches the story of the book and will be just the right atmosphere. The Main Hall and the carvery are within budget and you can provide some drinks. You don't think people will mind paying for any extra drinks. You really don't want canapés or a buffet wherever the event is – you think they look cheap. It has to be a sit-down meal or carvery.

Unit 6   page 61

Student B

Clarify what the customer's problem is.

Ask if they have tried your customer service line.

Apologise for the delay. Offer three months' free calls and promise to fix the phone immediately.

Unit 4 page 31

Student B

Has he always liked his job?	Yes, he has always liked his job
How long was he assistant manager for?	he worked as an assistant manager for 2 years
How many new stores has the company opened in the last five years?	The company has opened 25 stores in the last five years.

Unit 4 page 34

Student B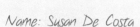

Name: Susan De Costa

Education: Bachelor's degree in hospitality management

Experience: She worked for two years in a hotel before moving to a chain of health clubs. She's helped make the health club one of the most popular in the region. She became manager in 2007. In 2008, she changed the club from a gym to health club. As a result, profits have increased 50%.

Skills: Bilingual in English and Spanish

Name: Jenny Flynn

Education: IGCSEs 8 Bs

Experience: She's worked in many hotels throughout Europe. She started as a trainee travel representative in 1991, and within two years was promoted to area manager. She's worked in customer service related departments of hotels. Her current hotel won a national award for the standards of its customer service in 2011. Jenny was given a lot of credit for the recruitment and training of her staff.

Skills: She's very culturally aware. She's lived and worked in many countries.

Unit 6 page 57

Student A

You work in customer service at OneTel Mobile. Deal with the customer's complaints by suggesting that he should have tried ringing at a different time as you get a lot of calls at this time.

Ask if he has sent any text messages this week.

Try to sell him a new phone.

Tell him the best thing to do is take the phone into a shop.

Unit 6 page 61

Student B

You're the manager of a restaurant and a customer isn't happy.

Apologise for the mistakes, but try to make an excuse – the chef is new, two waitresses were ill, the restaurant's very busy.

Unfortunately, you cannot offer a discount. The best you can do is give them a free coffee.

Unit 6 page 59

Student A

Customer loyalty by generation

Revenue Growth ($M)

Facebook — Groupon — Zynga — Google — Ebay — Yahoo — Amazon

Unit 6 page 62

Student B

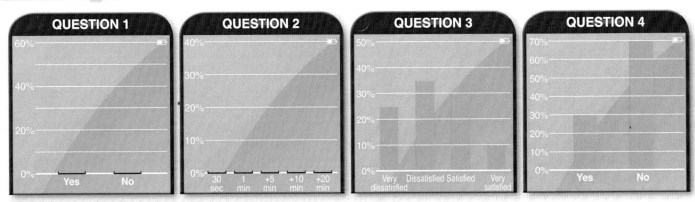

QUESTION 1	QUESTION 2	QUESTION 3	QUESTION 4
Yes No	30 sec / 1 min / +5 min / +10 min / +20 min	Very dissatisfied / Dissatisfied / Satisfied / Very satisfied	Yes No

Unit 8 page 73

Student B

You've been offered a new job and are negotiating the contract with your new employer. You want to negotiate salary, holiday and hours of work.

Salary: You want $150,000, but will accept as low as $120,000.

Holiday: You want 30 days, but know this is unlikely.

Hours of work: You want to work from home for one week a month; ideally a full week, but you'll take it over the month if you have to. You only want to work between 10.00 and 4.00 in the office. You'll work at home at other times, but your travel is cheaper and quicker going at these times.

Unit 8 page 79

Student B

You can't offer 15% on all the cars, but would offer 15% on the Skoda and 10% on the Prius.

You'll offer free insurance, but not free servicing.

You'll offer free seat adjustment and Bluetooth, but not satnav. It will cost £1,200 for the satnav.

The total bill is £370,968.

You can have some flexibility in the servicing – try to reach a deal.

Unit 9 page 87

Student B

You work for ToGo. You receive a call from Alto Café. They're not happy because they think an order was incorrect. When you look at the order, you see that they had only ordered fifteen and not 50. Alto Café are one of your most important customers. Decide what to do:

A Say sorry and then explain what happened and that it was their fault, not yours.

B Apologise. Don't mention their mistake and promise a discount on tomorrow's order.

C Apologise, but don't offer anything.

Unit 10 page 90

The well-travelled Sunday lunch

Chicken from Thailand	17,205 km by ship
Green beans from Zambia	7,905 km by plane
Carrots from Spain	1,609 km by lorry
Potatoes from Italy	2,447 km by lorry
Sprouts from Britain	201 km by lorry
Total	29,367 km

Unit 10 page 93

Student B

	Survey results	Survey comments
Money spent on green food products	$0 — 10% of people $1–$10 — 20% $11–$24 — 50% $25+ — 20%	1 ....
How often do you buy green food products?	2	Coffee and other snacks are the most common daily green purchase.
Most common green products bought	3	Local and seasonal vegetables were purchased most frequently.
Other green lifestyle choices	Cycling to work — 30% Recycling — 70% Energy-saving products for the home — 80% Holidaying in own country — 25%	4 ....
Age of green shoppers	5	Older generations were more concerned about quality and price.

Unit 4 page 35

The right person for the job

- The team were concerned about his lack of knowledge of the hospitality industry.
- They were concerned that he might not enjoy this new challenge and would move on again.
- They were concerned that he had no customer service experience.

Unit 10 page 95

Pair B

You're the directors of facilities management. Two employees have requested a meeting to suggest energy-saving initiatives. Try to think of the ideas they might suggest and what would be negative about these ideas from the company's point of view.

Unit 2 page 19

Student B

Salary and conditions

70% were satisfied with their salary.
68% were not satisfied with their working conditions.

Comments

Not getting a big pay rise I understood, but last year I worked hard and expected a good bonus.
We got bonuses every year so it became like our salary. Not getting a bonus was hard.

Unit 5 page 39

Student B

Provide recommendations to your partner. Then switch roles and ask your partner for recommendations on the following:

- delicious local dishes to eat
- shopping malls that aren't crowded
- exciting theatre shows to see.

Unit 6 page 57

Student B

You're a customer of OneTel Mobile. Complain about the following:

You've tried phoning five times.
You've been waiting on the phone for an hour.
You haven't received a text message for a week.

Ask what can be done to fix the phone.

Tell him you've been getting sales calls every day – you don't want a new phone.

You're slightly annoyed with his suggestion but do it anyway. Bye!

Unit 6 page 59

Student B

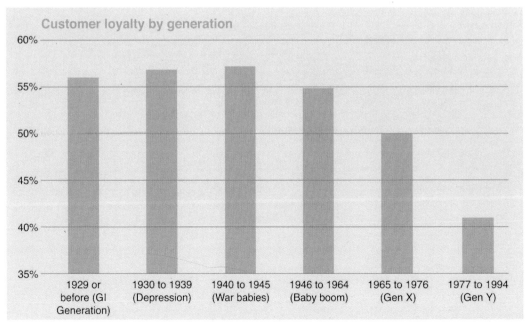

Customer loyalty by generation

Unit 3 page 26

Student C

The Baron

Serving traditional food with a modern twist, The Baron is an award-winning restaurant just off the main High Street. There has been a restaurant or bar in this location for over 200 years and the building still has many of its traditional features including open fires throughout the building. We have seating for up to 200 diners and rooms to accommodate 50 guests.

For large parties we recommend you pre-order one of our set menus:

Menu A £25 per head

Starters

Seasonal soup of the day, homemade bread [v]

Spring lamb meatballs, mint & cucumber yoghurt

Main courses

Catch of the day, potatoes, fried spring vegetables

Homemade spring vegetable flan, seasonal leaves, crispy croutons, house dressing [v]

Desserts

Homemade profiteroles, chocolate sauce

Classic crème brulée

Menu B £35 per head

Starters

Homemade vegetable spring rolls, mixed leaves, sweet chilli dressing [v]

Home smoked duck breast, red cabbage salad, balsamic syrup

Main courses

Beef fillet, cauliflower purée, potato & onions, seasonal mushrooms & parsley, red wine jus

Home made vegetable pie, white wine & herb crème fraiche, garlic mash [v]

Desserts

Trio of desserts

Cheese board

[v] = suitable for vegetarians   **Wine menu is available on request.**

Unit 2 page 19

Student C

Management and work-life balance

78% weren't happy with their work-life balance.

72% weren't happy with the management from their line manager.

Comments

I was working 35 hours a week two years ago. Now, I'm working 45 hours a week and get paid the same money.

I was making decisions in the past that my manager makes now. He gets paid more than I do for doing the same thing I was doing last year.

Unit 3 page 27

Student C

You'd like the expensive menu in the The Baron restaurant. The food is excellent and the location is great for people to get to. You think the bookshop is a terrible idea as everyone works in the book industry so they won't want to spend the night in a bookshop.

Grammar

Unit 1

Present simple with *He / She / It*

Full form	Questions	Short answers
Positive He / She / It works		
Negative He / She / It doesn't work	Does he / she / it work?	Yes, he / she / it does.
Wh- questions When does he go to work? Where does she need to go for the meeting? How does he travel to work? Who does she work with? What time does it start?	Does he / she / it start at nine? Does he / she / it finish at five?	No, he / she / it doesn't.

To make the third person singular:

a) most verbs   + *s*

Example:

live ▶ lives

b) verbs ending in *-s, -sh, -ch* or *-x*   + *es*

Examples:

kiss ▶ kisses, wish ▶ wishes, teach ▶ teaches, fix ▶ fixes

c) verbs ending in consonant + *y*   *y̶* + *ies*

Examples:

try ▶ tries, marry ▶ marries

d) verbs ending in vowel + *y*   + *s*

Examples:

say ▶ says, play ▶ plays

e) exceptions:

go ▶ goes, do ▶ does, have ▶ has

Use the present simple to talk about facts and routines.

Examples:

She lives in Hong Kong.

What does he do?

He works in a clothes shop. He works six days a week.

He doesn't work on Sundays.

What does she do?

She works for a design company. She uses a computer.

She doesn't work at weekends.

Present simple with *I / You / We / They*

Full form	Questions	Short answers
Positive I / You / We / They work		
Negative I / You / We / They don't work	Do I / you / we / they work on Sundays?	Yes, I / you / we / they do.
Wh- questions When do you go to work? Where do I go for a meeting? How do they travel to work? Who do you work with? What time do they start work?	Do I / you / we / they start at nine? Do I / you / we / they finish at five?	No, I / you / we / they don't.

Use the present simple to talk about:

a) things that are always true; facts.

Example:

We live in Tokyo.

Cows eat grass.

b) habits, routines, and things that occur repeatedly.

Examples:

I go to the gym every week.

They play football at the weekend.

Note:

These are the full forms of the negative verbs and the negative short answer.

I / You / We / They do not.

Only use these full forms:

a) in formal writing.

b) for emphasis.

Present simple *be*

Full form	Short form	Questions	Short answers	
Positive I am You / We / They are He / She / It is	**Positive** I'm You / We / They're He / She / It's	Am I hungry? Are you / we / they hungry? Is he / she / it hungry? Where are you from? When's dinner? What's the problem?	**Positive** Yes, I am. Yes, you are. Yes, he / she is. Yes, it is. Yes, we are. Yes, they are.	**Negative** No, I'm not. No, you aren't. No, he / she isn't. No, it isn't. No, we aren't No, they aren't.
Negative I am not You / We / They are not He / She / It is not	**Negative** I'm not You / We / They aren't He / She / It isn't			

When we speak we generally use short forms.
Use full forms:
a) in questions. Example:
Are you a student?
b) in positive short answers.
Example:
Yes, I am.

c) with names or words that end in *s*.
Example:
James is an engineer. This is my colleague.
Use full forms also:
a) in formal writing. Example:
Dear Mr Smith, We are very pleased to inform you that …
b) for emphasis. Example:
Susan's colleague: Susan isn't here.
Susan: I am here!

Present continuous

Full form	Questions	Short answers	
Positive I'm working. You / We / They're working. He / She / It's working.	Am I working? Are you / we / they working? Is he / she / it working?	**Positive** Yes, I am. Yes, you / we / they are. Yes, he / she / it is.	**Negative** No, I'm not. No, you / we / they / aren't. No, he / she / it isn't.
Negative I'm not working. You / We / They aren't working. He / She / It isn't working.			

Note:
These are the full forms of the positive and negative verbs.
I am working.
You / We / They are working.
He / She / It is working.
I am not working.
You / We / They are not working.
He / She / It is not working.

Only use these full forms:
a) in formal writing.
b) for emphasis.

Use the present continuous to describe temporary activities

The trains aren't running this week.
We aren't taking the bus today.
Are you cycling to work this morning?

Use the present continuous to talk about what you're doing at the moment.
Example:
What are you doing?
I'm watching a film.

Use time expressions like *at the moment, today* and *now* with the present continuous.

Spelling rules for -*ing* verbs
1 With most verbs simply add -*ing* to the verb.
   Examples:
   do ▶ doing, read ▶ reading, walk ▶ walking
2 When a verb has one syllable and ends with a consonant–vowel–consonant combination, double the last consonant and add -*ing* to the verb.
   Examples:
   run ▶ running, put ▶ putting, swim ▶ swimming
3 When the verb ends in an -*e* drop the -*e* and add -*ing* to the verb.
   Examples:
   have ▶ having, take ▶ taking, come ▶ coming

Verbs not usually used in the continuous

state verbs:

be, seem, have

thinking verbs:

know, understand, believe

emotion verbs:

like, love, hate, want

sense verbs:

see, taste, feel

Examples:

~~He is seeming~~ nervous during interviews. ▶ He seems nervous during interviews.

~~I am knowing~~ her because we go to school together. ▶ I know her because …

~~I am not liking~~ the film so I am leaving the cinema. ▶ I don't like the film so …

Some of these verbs can be used in the continuous with a special meaning:

I am thinking of buying a house (= planning)

Are you feeling OK? (= experiencing a sensation)

Unit 2

Past simple – regular forms

Full form	Questions	Short answers
Positive I / You / He / She / It / We / They worked. Negative I / You / He / She / It / We / They didn't work.	Did I / you / he / she / it / we / they work?	Yes, I / you / he / she / it / we / they did. No, I / you / he / she / it / we / they didn't.

Note:

These are the full forms of the negative verbs and the negative short answer.

I / You / He / She / It / We / They did not work.

No, I / you / he / she / it / we / they did not.

Only use these full forms:

a) in formal writing.

b) for emphasis.

Use the past simple to talk about events that happened in the past.

Spelling rules for regular past simple verbs

Most of the spelling rules for -ed are the same as for -ing. There is one additional rule. When a verb ends in a consonant + y, drop the y, add an i and then add ed.

Example:

try ▶ tried

Past simple – irregular forms

Some past simple verbs are irregular and they have an irregular past simple form.

Examples:

go ▶ went, have ▶ had.

Full form	Questions	Short answers
Positive I / You / He / She / It / We / They went to the mountains. Negative I / You / He / She / It / We / They didn't go to the mountains.	Did I / you / he / she / it / we / they go to the mountains?	Yes, I / you / he / she / it / we / they did. No, I / you / he / she / it / we / they didn't.

Note:

These are the full forms of the negative verbs and the negative short answer.

I / You / He / She / It / We / They did not go.

No, I / you / he / she / it / we / they did not.

Only use these full forms:

a) in formal writing.

b) for emphasis.

The verb can is a special case. The past simple of can is could. We form the negative with couldn't.

Example:

He could ride a bike, but he couldn't drive a car.

The past of have or has is had.

The past of get is got.

The past of do or does is did.

See the list of irregular verbs on page 114.

Past continuous

Full form	Short form	Questions	Short answers
Positive I / He / She / It was eating You / We / They were eating		Positive Was I / he / she / it eating?	Positive Yes, I / he / she / it was. Yes, you / we / they were.
Negative I / He / She / It was not eating You / We / They were not eating	Negative I / He / She / It wasn't eating You / We / They weren't eating	Negative Were you / we / they eating?	Negative No, I / he / she / it wasn't. No, you / we / they weren't.

To make the *-ing* form:

a) most verbs   + *ing*

Example:

send ▶ sending

b) verbs ending in *-e*   *e* + *ing*

Example:

live ▶ living

c) verbs ending in one vowel double consonant + one consonant (except *-y*, *-w*)

Example:

stop ▶ stopping

Use the past continuous to talk about:

a) the background or context in a story; the main actions or events are in the past simple.

Example:

She was going out with Peter when she met David.

b) actions in progress at a certain time in the past.

Example:

I was watching television at 9.30 this morning.

c) actions in progress when another completed action happened; the completed action is in the past simple.

Example:

I was surfing the internet when my mother phoned.

Remember!

Use the past continuous for the background.

Use the past simple for the main event.

Unit 3

Comparatives and superlatives

		Adjective	Comparative	Superlative
Most one-syllable adjectives	+ *er* / *est*	cold	colder	the coldest
One-syllable adjectives ending in *-e*	+ *r* / *st*	late	later	the latest
One- and two-syllable adjectives ending in consonant + *y*	*y* + *ier* / *iest*	pretty	prettier	the prettiest
One-syllable adjectives ending in one vowel + one consonant (except *-y*, *-w*)	double consonant	fat	fatter	the fattest
Adjectives of two or more syllables	*more* / *the most* (or l*ess* / l*east*) + + adjective	beautiful	more beautiful	the most beautiful
Irregulars		good bad far	better worse farther / further	the best the worst the farthest / furthest

Comparative adjectives

a) Use comparative adjective + *than* to compare people or things.
Examples:
John's older than Jeanette.
Canada's bigger than the USA.

b) Use *a lot / much / far* or *a bit / a little* before comparative adjectives.
Examples:
Your work is much better than mine.
That book's a bit more boring than this one.

c) Compare quantity using *more / less* + uncountable noun or *more / fewer* + countable noun. Example:
Pasta has more calories than salad.
There are fewer potatoes on my plate than on yours.

Note:
In formal English say:
Gary is taller than I am / than she is.
In conversational English we usually say:
Gary's taller than me / than her.

Superlative adjectives

a) Use *the* + superlative adjective to compare a person or thing with everyone / thing else in a particular group.
Example:
John's the oldest (person) in the group.

b) We usually put *in* before the names of places or groups of people. In most other cases, use *of* after superlatives.
Examples:
Madrid's the biggest city in Spain.
I'm the youngest of three boys.

c) Use *by far* before superlative adjectives for emphasis.
Examples:
That was by far the best party this year.

d) Compare quantity using *the most / the least* + uncountable noun or *the most / the fewest* + countable noun.
Example:
Of all my friends, Sue has the least money.

Unit 4

Past simple

See Unit 2

Present perfect

Full form	Short form	Questions	Short answers
Positive I / You / We / They have lived He / She / It has lived	Positive I've / You've / We've / They've lived He's / She's / It's lived	Have I / you / we / they lived? Has he / she / it lived?	Positive Yes, I / you / we / they have. Yes, he / she / it has.
Negative I / You / We / They have not lived He / She / It has not lived	Negative I / You / We / They haven't lived He / She / It hasn't lived		Negative No, I / you / we / they haven't. No, he / she / it hasn't.

We form the present perfect with *have / has* + past participle (*travelled, been, done,* etc.).
The past participle of regular verbs is the same as the past simple form.
The past participle of irregular verbs is often different from the past simple form.
See the list of irregular verbs on page 114.

Use the present perfect:
a) to talk about finished actions that have some importance now; we think about the past and present together.
Examples:
I've lost my keys. (I don't have them now.)
He's cut his finger. (Look! You can see the blood now.)
We don't normally use the present perfect with finished time references.
Example:
I lost my keys yesterday.

b) to give news; use the present perfect when we first give the news, then the past simple to give more details.
Example:
I've had an accident. I fell down the stairs.

c) to describe an experience that happened some time in our life, without saying when it happened; to give more details use the past simple.
Examples:
I've been to Ibiza. I went last year and I had a great time.
I've travelled all over the world. I went to Brazil in May.

d) to describe an action that started in the past and continues into the present.
Examples:
JUNE ————————————> NOW
He's lived here since June.
(NOT He lives here since June.)
TEN YEARS AGO ————————————> NOW
I've known Ian for ten years.
(NOT I know Ian for ten years.)

Past simple or present perfect

Woody Allen has directed lots of great films.
(He's alive. I'm thinking of the past and present.)
Alfred Hitchcock directed lots of great films.
(He's dead. I'm thinking of the past only.)
I've met lots of interesting people.
(Time not specified.)
I saw John yesterday.
(With specific times: *ago*, *in 1999*, etc.)
They've bought a new house.
(To give news.)
It cost a lot more than their flat.
(To give more details.)

Unit 5

Modal verbs

have to / don't have to

Full form	Questions	Short answers
Positive I / You / He / She / It / We / They have to Negative I / You / He / She / It / We / They don't have to	Do I / you / he / she / it / we / they have to?	Yes, I / you / he / she / it / we / they do. No, I / you / he / she / it / we / they don't.

Use *have to* to say that something is necessary.
Example:
I have to wear a uniform to work.
Use *don't have to* to say that something isn't necessary.
Example:
You don't have to do it if you don't want to.
Use *can't* to say that something is not allowed.
Example:
You can't park your car here.

must / mustn't

Full form	Short form	Questions	Short answers
Positive I / You / He / She / It / We / They must go		Must I / you / he / she / it / we / they go?	Positive Yes, I / you / he / she / it / we / they must.
Negative I / You / He / She / It / We / They must not go	Negative I / You / He / She / It / We / They mustn't go		Negative No, I / you / he / she / it / we / they mustn't.

Note:

must does not have an infinitive or a past participle (NOT to ~~must~~ / ~~I've musted~~).
a) Use *must* when we mean 'you are obliged to' or 'this is important'.
Example:
I must remember my mother's birthday this year.
b) However, we normally use *have to*, not *must*, to talk about rules and laws.
Example:
You have to be twenty-one to buy alcohol in the United States.
c) Use *mustn't* when we mean 'this is not allowed' or 'it's important that you don't'.
Example:
I mustn't lose my car keys.

Remember!
I have to / must buy some stationery.
(= I need to buy some.)
I don't have to buy any stationery.
(= I don't need to buy any. I already have enough.)
I mustn't buy any new stationery.
(= I'm not allowed to buy any. It's too expensive.)

should / shouldn't

Full form	Short form	Questions	Short answers
Positive I / You / He / She / It / We / They should go		Should I / you / he / she / it / we / they go?	Positive Yes, I / you / he / she / it / we / they should.
Negative I / You / He / She / It / We / They should not go	Negative I / You / He / She / It / We / They shouldn't go		Negative No, I / you / he / she / it / we / they shouldn't.

Use *should* when we mean 'it is a good idea' or 'it is a good thing to do'.
Example:
You should study hard before your exams.
We often use *should* to give advice.
Examples:
You should visit the Louvre when you're in Paris.
You shouldn't smoke if you're pregnant.

Remember!
Use *have to* to talk about what's necessary (obligation).
Use *should* to talk about what's a good idea.

Unit 6

Present perfect simple & present perfect continuous

Present perfect simple

Full form	Questions	Short answers
Positive I / You / We / They have ('ve) worked here. He / She / It has ('s) worked here.	Have I / you / we / they worked here? Has he / she / it worked here?	Yes, I / you / we have. Yes, he / she / it / has.
Negative I / You / We / They have not (haven't) worked here. He / She / It has not (hasn't) worked here.		No, I / you / we have not (haven't). No, he / she / it / has not (hasn't).

See the list of irregular verbs on page 114

Present perfect continuous

Full form	Questions	Short answers
Positive I / You / We / They have ('ve) been working here since June. He / She / It has ('s) been working here since June.	Have I / you / we / they been working here since June? Has he / she / it been working here since June?	Yes, I / you / we have. Yes, he / she / it / has.
Negative I / You / We / They have not (haven't) been working here since June. He / She / It has not (hasn't) been working here since June?		No, I / you / we have not (haven't). No, he / she / it / has not (hasn't).

Use the present perfect simple to talk about:
a) actions / states that began in the past and continue in the present.
Example:
I've been here for half an hour.

b) completed actions or activities that are relevant at the moment of speaking:
Examples:
Sam's done four exams this week.
I've finished typing it up – shall I print it?

Use the present perfect continuous to talk about:
a) actions / activities that began in the past and continue in the present.
Example:
Gisela has been studying English for eight years.
b) recently completed activities or processes that are relevant at the moment of speaking:
Example:
Drive carefully, it's been raining.

The present perfect simple and the present perfect continuous are sometimes interchangeable:
I've lived here for ten years.
I've been living here for ten years.

Use the simple form to emphasise the result or completion of the activity:
I've done my homework (so now I'm doing something else).

Use the continuous form to emphasise the process, or incompletion, of the activity:
I've been doing my homework. (That's why I was in my room.)

To talk about the number of times we have done something, use the present perfect simple:
I've written ten postcards this morning.

To talk about the duration of an activity, we often use the present perfect continuous:
I've been writing postcards all morning.

Note that the continuous form is not usually used with:
state verbs:
be, seem, have;
thinking verbs:
know, understand, believe;
emotion verbs:
like, love, hate;
except when these verbs express activities:
I've been having three children.
I've been having a shower.

Unit 7

will

Full form	Short form	Questions	Short answers
Positive I / You / He / She / It / We / They will go	Positive I'll / You'll / He'll / She'll / It'll / We'll / They'll go	Will I / you / he / she / it / we / they go?	Positive Yes, I / you / he / she / it / we / they will.
Negative I / You / He / She / It / We / They will not go	Negative I / You / He / She / It / We / They won't go		Negative No, I / you / he / she / it / we / they won't.

Use *will* to refer to future time:
Examples:
The elections will take place on 26th July.
I will be forty on my next birthday.

Predictions
Use *will* + infinitive to say what we think or know about the future.
Example:
It'll probably rain tomorrow.
We often make predictions with *I think + will* or *I expect + will*.
Example:
I think AC Milan will win the match.

going to

Full form	Short form	Questions	Short answers
Positive I am going to play You / We / They are going to play He / She / It is going to play	Positive I'm / You're / He's / She's / It's / We're / They're going to play	Am I going to play? Are you / we / they going to play? Is he / she / it going to play?	Positive Yes, I am. Yes, you / we / they are. Yes, he / she / it is.
Negative I am not going to play You / We / They are not going to play He / She / It is not going to play	Negative I'm not going to play You / We / They aren't going to play He / She / It isn't going to play		Negative No, I'm not. No, you / we / they aren't. No, he / she / it isn't.

Predictions

a) Use *going to* when a future event is evident.
Examples:
Look at that guy! He's going to fall!
Look! That car is going to crash!
b) We can also use *going to* like *will*, to make predictions.
Examples:
I think it's going to rain this evening.
You're going to love that film.
c) But when we talk about conditions, use *will* to make predictions.
Examples:
If you buy that flat, you won't regret it.
If you don't revise, you'll fail the exam.

Plans

a) Use *going to* to talk about intentions and plans that we have already made.
Examples:
I'm going to have a holiday next week.
He's going to work abroad.
b) But use the present continuous to talk about plans and arrangements in the future which are sure to happen.
Often there is a definite time and / or place for arrangements in the present continuous.
Example:
I'm catching the 6.00 p.m. train tomorrow.

Present continuous

Use the present continuous to talk about fixed plans and arrangements in the future. There is often a definite time or place, and we have often agreed with somebody else / written it in our diaries.
Examples:
I'm meeting Carmen for lunch tomorrow.
My sister's getting married next year.

Remember!
I'm going to have a coffee with Sean one day soon.
I'm having a coffee with Sean in the local café at 10.00.

Unit 8

Zero conditional

If + present simple, present simple

Use the zero conditional to talk about scientific laws and other things that are always true.
Example:
If you heat ice, it melts.

First conditional

If + present simple + *will*

Examples:
If it's rainy tomorrow, we'll stay at home. (NOT If it will be rainy)
If you come late, I'll wait for you. (NOT If you will come)
a) With *if*, use present tenses to talk about possible or probable events in the future. We often use the present simple tense after *if*.

Example:

If I go to LA, I'll visit my friend Patrick.

b) You can change the order of conditional sentences.

Example:

If I go to LA, I'll visit my friend Patrick. = I'll visit my friend Patrick if I go to LA.

c) We can use *unless* to mean *if ... not*.

Example:

If you don't drive fast, we'll miss the train. = Unless you drive fast, we'll miss the train.

Note:

We can use the present simple in both the *if* clause and the main clause to refer to general truths and facts.

Example:

If I feel tense, I go for a run.

We can also use other present tenses after *if*.

Examples:

If you're going to the shops, will you buy me some milk?

If you haven't done this before, I will help you.

We can also use other modal verbs or the imperative instead of *will*.

Examples:

If it's rainy tomorrow, we should stay at home.

If it's rainy tomorrow, come round to our house.

Second conditional

If + past simple + *would*

Use the second conditional to talk about things which are impossible or unlikely to happen in the present / future and their consequences.

Examples:

If it snowed in summer, people wouldn't go to the beach.

If I met the president tomorrow, I'd tell him to spend more money on poor people.

We can use *were* instead of *was*. This is very common when we use the second conditional to give advice.

Example:

If I were you, I'd go and see a doctor.

We can also use other modals instead of would.

Example:

If we lived somewhere else, we might be happier.

Sometimes both the first and second conditional can be possible, depending on the level of probability.

Examples:

If we win the match tomorrow, we'll be champions.

If I had a lot of money, I'd buy a big house in the country.

Unit 9

Past simple

Full form	Questions	Short answers
Positive I / He / She / It slept. You / We /They slept.	Did I / he / she / it sleep? Did you / we / they sleep?	**Positive** Yes, I / he / she / it did. Yes, you / we / they did.
Negative I / He / She / It did not (didn't) sleep. You /We /They did not (didn't) sleep.		**Negative** No, I / he / she / it didn't. No, you / we / they didn't.

See the list of irregular verbs on page 114.

Use the past simple to talk about: past habits, events and states.

Examples:

We went camping every summer when I was a child.

He got up at 7.00 a.m., had breakfast and went to work.

I thought you loved me.

Past continuous

Full form	Questions	Short answers
Positive I / He / She / It was sleeping. You / We /They were sleeping.	Was I / he / she / it sleeping? Were you / we / they sleeping?	**Positive** Yes, I / he / she / it was. Yes, you / we / they were.
Negative I / He / She / It was not (wasn't) sleeping. You /We /They were not (weren't) sleeping.		**Negative** No, I / he / she / it wasn't. No, you / we / they weren't.

Use the past continuous to talk about:
actions in progress in the past.
Examples:
I was reading a book last night.
At 8.00 a.m. Robin was cycling to work.
These actions can be:
a) interrupted.
Example:
I was watching a film when the doorbell rang.
b) the background to another event.

Example:
Inside the club, music was playing and people were singing and dancing. We sat down at a table ...
c) simultaneous.
Example:
While Gloria and Pablo were cooking dinner, Cristina was playing with the children.

Past perfect

Full form	Short form	Questions	Short answers
Positive I / You / He / She / It / We / They had lived	Positive I'd / You'd / He'd / She'd / It'd / We'd / They'd lived	Had I / you / he / she / it / we / they lived?	Positive Yes, I / you / he / she / it / we / they had.
Negative I / You / He / She / It / We / They had not lived	Negative I / You / He / She / It / We / They hadn't lived		Negative No, I / you / he / she / it / we / they hadn't.

We form the past perfect with *had* + past participle (*travelled, been, done*, etc.).
The past participle of regular verbs is the same as the past simple form.
The past participle of irregular verbs is often different from the past simple form.
See the list of irregular verbs on page 114.

Use the past perfect:
a) when we are talking about the past and want to talk about an earlier past time.
Examples:
He was sad because he had lost his job.
(PAST)   (EARLIER PAST)
When we got to the station, the train had already left.
(PAST)   (EARLIER PAST)
b) after *when* / *after* to show that something is finished.
Examples:
When Tony had finished dinner, he went to bed.
After we had tidied up the flat, we watched TV.

Unit 10

The passive

Active: People speak English in New Zealand.
Passive: English is spoken in New Zealand.
In the active sentence, the topic is the people. In the passive sentence, the topic is English.
We form the passive voice with the verb *to be* + past participle (*finished, sent, done*, etc.)

The passive is used to focus on when, where or what was done rather than who did it.

Full form	Short form	Questions	Short answers
Positive I am paid You / We / They are paid He / She / It is paid	Positive I'm / You're / He's / She's / It's / We're / They're paid	Am I paid? Are you / we / they paid? Is he / she / it paid?	Positive Yes, I am. Yes, you / we / they are. Yes, he / she / it is.
Negative I / You / He / She / It / We / They had not paid	Negative I'm not paid You / We / They aren't paid He / She / It isn't paid		Negative No, I'm not. No, you / we / they aren't. No, he / she / it isn't.

Use the present simple passive to talk about routines and facts (things that are always true).
Examples:
I am paid every month (by my company).
Coca-Cola is sold in almost every country in the world.

Past simple passive

Full form	Short form	Questions	Short answers
Positive I / He / She / It was paid You / We / They were paid		Was I / he / she / it paid? Were you / we / they paid?	Positive Yes, I / he / she / it was. Yes, you / we / they were.
Negative I / He / She / It was not paid You / We / They were not paid	Negative I / He / She / It wasn't paid You / We / They weren't paid		Negative No, I / he / she / it wasn't. No, you / we / they weren't.

Use the past simple passive to talk about completed or finished actions and events.
Examples:
This house was built in the last century.
My purse was stolen last night.
The match was won by Germany.

Present perfect passive

Full form	Short form	Questions	Short answers
Positive I / You / We / They have been paid. He / She / It has been paid.	Positive I've / You've / We've / They've been paid. He's / She's / It's been paid.	Have I / you / we / they been paid? Has he / she / it been paid?	Positive Yes, I / you / we / they have. Yes, he / she / it has.
Negative I / You / We / They have not been paid. He / She / It has not been paid.	Negative I / You / We / They haven't been paid. He / She / It hasn't been paid.		Negative No, I / he / she / it wasn't. No, you / we / they weren't.

Use the present perfect simple passive to talk about completed actions that are relevant now.
Examples:
New laws have been introduced by the government.
The football match has been cancelled.
This year's Oscar nominees have been announced.

Present continuous passive

Full form	Short form	Questions	Short answers
Positive I am being paid. You / We / They are being paid. He / She / It is being paid.	Positive I'm being paid. You're / We're / They're being paid. He's / She's / It's being paid.	Are I / you / we / they being paid?	Positive Yes, I am. Yes, you / we / they are. Yes, he / she / it is.
Negative I / You / We / They are not being paid. He / She / It is not being paid.	Negative I / You / We / They aren't being paid. He / She / It isn't being paid.	Is he / she / it being paid?	Negative No, I'm not. No, you / we / they aren't. No, he / she / it isn't.

Use the present continuous passive to talk about activities or processes in progress at the moment of speaking.
Examples:
They're being given instructions by the director.
She's being paid for her work.
Are you being treated fairly?

Irregular verbs

Infinitive	Past simple	Past participle
be	was, were	been
become	became	become
begin	began	begun
bite	bit	bitten
break	broke	broken
bring	brought	brought
build	built	built
buy	bought	bought
catch	caught	caught
choose	chose	chosen
come	came	come
cost	cost	cost
do	did	done
dream	dreamt/dreamed	dreamt/dreamed
drink	drank	drunk
drive	drove	driven
eat	ate	eaten
fall	fell	fallen
feel	felt	felt
fight	fought	fought
find	found	found
fly	flew	flown
forbid	forbade	forbidden
forget	forgot	forgotten
forgive	forgave	forgiven
get	got	got/gotten (US)
give	gave	given
go	went	gone
grow	grew	grown
have	had	had
hear	heard	heard
hide	hid	hidden
hit	hit	hit
hold	held	held
hurt	hurt	hurt
keep	kept	kept
know	knew	known
lead	led	led
learn	learnt/learned	learnt/learned
leave	left	left
let	let	let
light	lit/lighted	lit/lighted
lose	lost	lost
make	made	made
meet	met	met
pay	paid	paid
put	put	put

Infinitive	Past simple	Past participle
read /riːd/	read /red/	read /red/
ride	rode	ridden
ring	rang	rung
rise	rose	risen
run	ran	run
say	said	said
see	saw	seen
sell	sold	sold
send	sent	sent
set	set	set
shake	shook	shaken
shoot	shot	shot
show	showed	shown/showed
shut	shut	shut
sing	sang	sung
sit	sat	sat
sleep	slept	slept
smell	smelt/smelled	smelt/smelled
speak	spoke	spoken
spend	spent	spent
spill	spilt/spilled	spilt/spilled
spread	spread	spread
stand	stood	stood
steal	stole	stolen
stick	stuck	stuck
stink	stank/stunk	stunk
strike	struck	struck
swear	swore	sworn
sweep	swept	swept
swell	swelled	swollen/swelled
swim	swam	swum
swing	swung	swung
take	took	taken
teach	taught	taught
tear	tore	torn
tell	told	told
think	thought	thought
throw	threw	thrown
understand	understood	understood
upset	upset	upset
wake	woke	woken
wear	wore	worn
weep	wept	wept
wet	wet/wetted	wet/wetted
win	won	won
write	wrote	written
wet	wet/wetted	wet/wetted
win	won	won
write	wrote	written

Audioscripts

Unit 1

1.1

It's a hard job physically, but then I wouldn't want an office job – it would drive me crazy! I love being outside and it keeps me fit. I usually cycle between 50 and 100 miles every day. We generally work from nine to six, but today I'm working from nine to five as I have a friend's birthday to go to tonight.
I normally take a thirty-minute lunch break when I have time, but because I'm finishing early, I'm not taking one today.
We mostly carry small envelopes and files for the press, media companies and legal firms. We used to do a lot for banks, but not so much now. Today I have an unusual delivery: I'm taking some clothes to a fashion designer.
The business is having a difficult time at the moment. I normally earn £200 per week, but this week has been very busy and I will probably earn £600. In the past, that was normal, but more things are sent electronically now.
Most days I enjoy riding for work, but like everything there are days when it's no fun – like today when it's raining. But I couldn't imagine being in an office every day.

1.2

Hi. My name's Jan Bergstrom and I work for FIB manufacturing. Our company runs quite a long manufacturing day so we have a number of different shift managers. I'm the first shift manager so I work early in the mornings. The second shift manager, Richard Smith, runs the next shift and Yumi Nohara's the third shift manager. Our line manager is Tatsuki Sano, and he's the factory manager. We report directly to him and he's responsible for the overall running of the factory. Working alongside Tatsuki is Edda Lunberg, who's responsible for the engineering side of things and Rachel Skinner, who's the quality control manager. We have five directors responsible for different departments. Firstly, there's Aleksej Lindström, who's the director of research and development. The director of marketing is Sally Manning. Taka Akita is the director of manufacturing. He's in charge of our department overall and is the line manager of my boss Tatsuki. Responsible for all money matters is Domar Lindgren, the director of finance. And Oli Richards is our director of human resources. Then at the top of the company is the president, Aksel Lindberg.

1.3

I work for FIB manufacturing – based in Sweden, but very much an international company. I'm a shift manager and work in the main factory from 6 a.m. till 2 p.m. I work alongside two other shift managers and I report to Tasuki Sano, the factory manager. I have two main responsibilities. Firstly, I'm in charge of twenty production assistants. It's my responsibility to look after all the machinery and factory staff. If any problems occur, I have to deal with them. We have targets to meet each day and I'm responsible for my team meeting these targets.

1.4

1
P = Paul, O = operators (1, 2 and 3)
P: I'd like to speak to somebody about my last bill, please.
O1: One moment. I'll just put you through.
O2: Good day sir, I understand you'd like to pay your bill.
P: No, I have a problem with my bill.

O2: I'm sorry, you need another department. One moment. I'll just put you through.
O3: Good afternoon sir, how can I help?
P: There are some calls on my bill I don't think I made.
O3: Sorry sir, you need …
P: All I need is someone to help me! Ahh!

2
A = Arabella, J = Jane
A: Could I speak to Sven Carlson, please?
J: I'm afraid he's out of the office. Can I help at all?
A: Thank you, but I really need to speak to him directly.
J: Can I take a message?
A: Could you ask him to call me when he's back?
J: Certainly.

3
U = Ulrike, O = operator
U: Could I speak to somebody in accounts, please?
O: I'm afraid everyone's in a meeting at the moment. Would you like to leave a message?
U: No, it's fine. I'll call back later.

1.5

A = Alicia, O = operator
A: Can I speak to Sergio Tevez, please?
O: Certainly. Can I ask who's calling?
A: It's Alicia Zola.
O: Certainly, can you hold on a moment? I'll just put you through.
A: Sure.
O: I'm afraid he's not there at the moment. Can I take a message?
A: Can you ask him to call me back?
O: Of course, can you tell me your name again, please?
A: It's Alicia Zola.
O: Sorry, can you say that again, please?

1.6

1 Can I ask who's calling?
2 Can you hold on a moment?
3 Can I take a message?
4 Can you ask him to call me back?
5 Can you tell me your name again, please?
6 Can you say that again, please?

1.7

1
L = Louis, O = operator
L: Hi, could I speak to Fiona Watson, please?
O: I'm afraid she's not in at the moment. Would you like me to ask her to call you back?
L: Yes, if you don't mind. Could you ask her to call Louis Eliot on 972 8733?
O: Is that with one L in the middle or two?
L: One L and Louis is spelt L-O-U-I-S, not L-E-W-I-S.
O: Great. Did you say your number is 972 8773?
L: No, sorry it's 972 8733. It's about our latest order.
O: OK, I'll ask Fiona to call you back.

2
A = Andrew, O = operator
A: Hi, this is Andrew Newton. Could I speak to Connie Wood, please?
O: I'm sorry, I didn't catch your name.
A: Sorry, it's Andrew Newton.
O: Where did you say you're calling from?

A: Peel Ltd.

O: Sorry, could you spell it, please?

A: It's P-E-E-L.

O: Is that P for Paul or B for Bertie?

A: P for Paul.

O: OK, one minute – I'll just connect you ... I'm afraid she's out. Could I ask why you're calling?

A: I'd just like to ask her about a course that you have starting soon. Could you ask her to ring me back on 01568 926629?

O: Certainly.

))) 1.8

F = Fiona, L = Louis

F: Hi, could I speak to Louise Eliot, please?

L: Sorry, do you mean Louis Eliot?

F: Oh dear, sorry yes. How embarrassing!

L: Don't worry about it. My own aunt spells it L-O-I-S. How can I help?

))) 1.9

Richmond Design Solutions is a successful graphic design company. They design websites, logos, and marketing products for several important companies. The administration department at Richmond Design Solutions has a total of nine employees. Fredrik Sandgren is the new Administration Manager. He takes over from Martina Strand – who's leaving the company after ten years. Two senior administrators report to Fredrik directly; Svenja Hansen and Katja Gruenenberg. They look after the company's key customers and they deal with all legal contracts. They also provide admin services to the four design project managers. There are then four general administrators: Jessica Braun and Björn Eklund, who report to Svenja, and Christina Gunnarson and Stella Nilsson who report to Katja. Jessica and Björn are in charge of meeting room bookings, catering, and business trip arrangements. Christina and Stella deal with the admin for the ten designers on the design team. Finally, there are two junior administrators: Holly Olsson, who reports to Björn and Johanna Vang, who reports to Stella. The junior administrators answer all phone calls and email enquiries, deal with new customers, and order stationery for the office.

))) 1.10

K = Karin, F = Fredrik

K: So if we were to offer you the position, how could you help the department?

F: I think my main role would be assessing what current staff do and looking to make changes.

K: Do you have any specific ideas in mind?

F: Well, in my last company we made a change so that no one had a specific role or job title – they simply prioritised what they needed to do.

K: Isn't that quite difficult to manage?

F: It can be, but if you define tasks clearly and train staff well, it can really help.

K: What training do you think the staff would need?

F: Well, if someone is an expert on computer systems but does little customer telephone work, then you give them training in customer service skills and telephone handling. Basically, you want people to do more than just one simple role.

K: What's the benefit to the company? Surely it's better to have experts?

F: It can be, but it's also good to have staff that are flexible. It means the company can manage changes in workloads better. You don't have the situation where in one office three people are very busy and three are checking Facebook.

K: How would you make this work in practice?

F: It's about changing people's working methods. People don't have set tasks to do; the department has set tasks to do. It means everyone knows how to do a range of tasks and can help each other more.

))) 1.11

B = Björn, C = Christina, J = Jessica

B: So what do you think of our new boss, Christina?

C: He's nice, very friendly.

B: True, but what about all the changes he's making?

C: I think they're good. It's harder work, but more interesting and fun.

B: I can never leave early now!

C: I never could ... What do you think, Jessica?

J: It is fairer now, but this isn't the job I was employed to do. I like dealing with travel arrangements and organising meetings. I've got a really good relationship with our travel agency and I'm really good at making sure meetings are well organised with the best food and drink. I'm not good with new customers. I hate having to answer the phone! It was better when Holly and Johanna took all the phone calls.

C: They do provide training.

J: I know, but you can't train people to be good on the phone with new people. It's not a natural thing for me. I don't mind working harder, but I don't want to answer the phone.

B: I hate all the training. I spend so much time being trained I don't have enough time to do my job. The training to do the legal contracts was so hard! And Svenja and Katja really weren't happy about us learning how to do them!

C: But it's good – it'll make us more skilled.

B: True ... then I can get a better job in another company!

C: You wouldn't leave, would you?

B: Maybe ...

J: You know, my holiday got refused for next month. Apparently, we're too busy next month because it's the end of the financial year, so no holidays for anyone.

C: But I always take a holiday in June! I take it every year.

J: Well, not this year you're not.

C: I'm not putting up with that. I'm going to complain to Karin.

B: Ha! Good. I knew there'd be something you didn't like.

))) 1.12

K = Karin, F = Fredrik

K: Fredrik, you started a month ago now and I thought this would be a good time to catch up.

F: Sure.

K: How do you think the changes are going?

F: I'm really happy with them. Some of the team, especially the ones who have been here a long time, are finding it hard, but some like Christina and Holly are great.

K: Yes, we're pleased with how you're settling in and some of the changes have been good.

F: I sense a 'but' coming.

K: Well, a couple of things. Some of the designers have said that when they try to contact a member of your team, they're often busy.

F: They could be, but they could also always speak to someone else in the team. That's part of the point of the changes. Now many people can do each task.

K: Yes, but that's also one of the problems. Nobody knows who they should contact about what now. Even our key customers are confused by the new system – which is not good.

F: But they can contact anyone in the team.

K: Yes, but this needs to be communicated clearly to the designers and the customers. Things are not being done because people aren't answering messages. No one's taking responsibility for tasks. Svenja and Katja are frustrated that they can't look after our key customers and they're also unhappy that the others are being trained to deal with contracts. I think we might need to go back to the old system, this all seems a bit chaotic to me. And Holly and Johanna are asking for more money as they now have a lot more responsibilities!

F: No, no. These are all minor problems, we can sort them out.

K: They're not minor Fredrik, work isn't being done, no one knows who does what and your team isn't happy! It needs to get sorted out soon!

Unit 2

))) 2.1

Kerstin

I got a great job after university. We earned a lot of money and the company were always giving us bonuses. Many people loved the lifestyle, but we worked such long hours. Often just when I was leaving, my boss gave me more work to do. We made good money so this was OK, but some people were not given as much work to do and my boss was always giving me too much work so I left.

Marco

I worked in a market research call centre while I was studying at university. It was a difficult job because people thought we were trying to sell them something, but we only wanted to find out their opinion. I just left one day in the middle of a phone call. A person was shouting at me on the phone and I just quit on the spot.

Sven

My worst job ever? This time last year, I was working long hours for not much money and found it very stressful. I decided the money wasn't worth the stress and quit.

))) 2.2

fire   resign
ladder   appraisal
assess   career
promote   retire

))) 2.3

N = Nina, G = Gareth

N: I'm glad to see you're happy with the past year, Gareth. Overall, we think your work is excellent.

G: I'm really happy. I think things are going really well.

N: Yes, definitely! So your biggest achievement this year is your accounts management. Could you explain a little bit more?

G: Sure, this year I took on one of our key accounts and the feedback has been very positive. We keep getting repeat orders and I think this is helped by the way I've managed the account.

N: We're really pleased. Your contribution here means that we've been able to expand our sales and meet our targets. So I see you like the amount of responsibility you have, but not the administration workload.

G: I really enjoy being responsible for projects and get a lot of satisfaction meeting targets, but yes, I don't enjoy the paperwork.

N: Do you find the paperwork difficult?

G: No, it's not difficult to do the paperwork, what I find most difficult is having the time to do it.

N: You're doing really well, so keep it up, but perhaps we can look to get you some more administrative support. I'm particularly pleased with the way you manage your team so I'd be very happy to expand it. I see one of your main aims is to improve your sales skills. Why do you think this is important for you?

G: Well, I think I'm good at keeping key customers happy, but I think I also have the skills, with some training, to help expand our customer base.

N: I would agree one of your key strengths is keeping customers happy. You've done a good job there, but we could always benefit from building on markets, so if you could help add to this, that would be excellent. Also I see you'd like to be a regional manager in three years' time and to achieve this, you do need to have more sales experience.

))) 2.4

1 Overall, we think your work is excellent.
2 Your contribution here means that we've been able to expand our sales and meet our targets.
3 You're doing really well so keep it up, but perhaps we can look to get you some more administrative support.
4 I'm particularly pleased with the way you manage your team so I'd be very happy to expand it.
5 One of your key strengths is keeping customers happy.
6 You've done a good job there, but we could always benefit from building on markets, so if you could help add to this, that would be excellent.

))) 2.5

A: Well, this was a bit of a disaster then, wasn't it?
B: I know. I thought our staff were happy!
A: Well, it's not all bad. People were happy with their career path – they just don't think they have any chance of promotion now.
B: When we were paying bonuses, everyone was obviously happy, but then we stopped.
A: The salaries satisfied most people.
B: Yes, but for how long? No one was pleased with their work-life balance or their manager!

Unit 3

))) 3.1

make   avoid   weigh   decide   delay

))) 3.2

display   choice   provide

))) 3.3

1 I find it difficult to make decisions.
2 Why do you always avoid making decisions?
3 Did you weigh up the options carefully?
4 When do we have to decide by?
5 I don't think we should delay the decision any further.

))) 3.4

S = Sanjay, M = Meiko

S: So what do you think of this year's event?
M: It's OK, but it could be a lot better.
S: The food was certainly better last year. I think this is probably the worst food I've ever had at a conference.
M: Oh come on, it's not that bad. Don't you remember Brighton two years ago?

S: Oh yes! How could I forget? That really was the most disgusting food ever. The presenters were at least more interesting in Brighton. I could barely stay awake this morning!

M: Yeah, they're not great so far, are they? I'm at least looking forward to some events this afternoon. I found it really hard with the jet lag by the afternoon last year in Vancouver. I really was falling asleep then and not because the presentations were boring.

S: It was a nice idea to go to Vancouver last year. The venue is much more modern and bigger than here, but it's just too far to go.

M: I think it's the furthest from Europe the event has been. Everyone was exhausted! At least Athens is easier to get to than Brighton.

S: Yes, why they had it so far from an airport I don't know.

M: It's a really good number of people though. I think this is the busiest it's ever been.

S: Last year was probably busier, it's just the Vancouver venue was bigger than here.

3.5

M = Mona, A = Ahmed, C = Chintal

M: Right, so we need to get a range of hotels to offer to delegates. So what does everyone think?

A: From my perspective, we have to put the Myatt in the brochure. It's the nicest hotel in the town centre.

C: Really? I agree with you up to a point, but isn't it a little too expensive?

M: I couldn't agree more. The Madison is just as good, but about twenty per cent cheaper.

A: Yes, but it's a bit further from the venue and the food isn't as good.

C: I'm not sure about that. It is a bit further, but the food's not that bad.

A: OK, let's put the Madison in.

M: Well, that's one for the town centre. How about an airport one? How about City Travel or Flight Link?

C: As far as I'm concerned, it has to be City Travel. Flight Link is just terrible! OK, it's ...

A: ... much cheaper.

C: Yes, it's much cheaper, but the standard is so low.

M: Isn't it owned by that horrible budget flight company?

A: Sorry, but for some people, the price is the most important thing.

C: It's only $10 cheaper per night.

A: Remember we get a lot of students at this event. Price is the number one concern. I think we should put Flight Link in.

M: That's fine with me. Let's say it's a budget hotel in the programme! OK, so now a hotel for people who might stay for a holiday. Perhaps one with spa facilities. Parkside?

C: The drawback is the location.

M: It's in a beautiful park, amazing building, fantastic food, tennis ...

A: Sorry, but it's in the middle of nowhere. It would ...

M: Yes, but that's its charm.

A: It would take 25 minutes in the car every day or a lot of taxis.

C: How about the Berkeley?

M: Hardly the same as Parkside!

A: No, but more practical location and it does have a spa.

C: Yes, let's go for the Berkeley.

3.6

M = Miguel, K = Karen

M: So the launch is only three months away now.

K: Yes, we need to decide on a venue and get invitations sent out.

M: How many people are we inviting?

K: Around 200, I think. We'll maybe invite 250 but a maximum of 200 will come.

M: So shall we budget with 200 in mind?

K: Yes, let's do that. Well, we have £8,000 so we should be able to do something good.

M: Is that for food and drink?

K: No, it depends on the venue. Some charge a fee to hire. We might want music and other entertainment as well.

M: True, but I think we should spend no less than £20 per person on food and drink and if we can get a venue for free then £40 per head. Any ideas for venues?

K: Well, we could go for a bookstore – it'd be free.

M: How about the castle? The location is stunning.

K: Yes, we'd have to check venue costs though and isn't it a bit far out?

M: Maybe, we could look at The Baron restaurant. The food is excellent.

K: OK, let's do a bit more research on the costs and options of those three.

Unit 4

4.1

consulted	answered	checked
decided	emailed	laughed
posted	played	pushed
wanted	stayed	shipped

4.2

I love working here! I started in 2007 and have loved everything about it: from the product to the building to my colleagues, I've loved everything. My first position was as a junior sales manager, which I did for two years. I was then promoted to assistant manager, which again I did for two years. I've been responsible for three different departments in the store: men's clothing, women's clothing and household goods. The company's growing fast and has opened five new stores every year for the last five years. Today, I'm the southern regional sales manager, which I've worked as for the last three years. This is the best company I've ever worked for.

4.3

1

C = Carolina, B = Beltina, M = Maria

C: Hi there. I was just wondering – have you met Maria?

B: No, I haven't. Nice to meet you.

M: Nice to meet you, too. You must be Bettina.

B: That's right.

C: I worked with Maria in Valencia two years ago.

B: Oh really? That's great. I love that city.

M: I had a great time there. It was a great job, great city and of course great colleagues like Carolina.

B: Yes, it's an amazing place, isn't it? Well, we've got quite a few people here at the conference. In fact, I'd like you both to meet Chad. He's a new sales rep in our team. You can have a chat with him about ...

2

C = Carolina, I = Isabel

C: Excuse me. May I join you?

I: Sure.

C: Are you on the flight to Milan?

I: Yes, I am. Are you?

C: Yep, I'm going for work.

I: Me too. What does your company do?

C: We publish school books.

I: Ahh, so you're going to the conference too! So, where does your company operate then?

C: Well, mainly in the UK, but we also sell books to international schools all around the world.

I: Oh, right – it sounds like it's an interesting company to work for.

C: Yeah, it's not bad. So…. what does your company do, then?

I: We publish history books – mainly dealing with South American history.

C: That sounds interesting – and where are you based?

I: In Recife.

3

C = Carolina, T = Tom

C: Hey, Tom – nice to see you again.

T: Good to see you again, too. I heard you were in our office this week. How's everything going?

C: Well, the team's really busy – as always, but apart from that I'm fine.

T: Yeah, I know the feeling. Are you going to a meeting?

C: No, I've just had one. I'm going to the café to buy myself a skinny latte.

T: I'd love a coffee, too. May I join you?

C: Sure …

))) 4.4

1	Nice to see you again.	Good to see you again, too.
2	Have you met Christiana?	No, I don't believe I have.
3	What does your company do?	We publish primary school books.
4	May I join you?	Sure.
5	I'd like you to meet Maria.	Nice to meet you.
6	How's everything going?	Not too bad, thanks.
7	You must be Lucy.	That's right.
8	Where are you based?	In Rio.
9	Where does your company operate?	We have branches across the whole of Latin America.

))) 4.5

1

P = Pedro, L = Laura

P: Hi there. Are you one of Carolina's colleagues?

L: Yes – how did you guess?

P: Erm, I'm not sure. I saw you talking a lot earlier and you seemed to know each other well.

L: How about you? How do you know Carolina?

P: I'm one of her former work colleagues.

L: So you're in publishing then?

P: Yes. What about you? What do you do?

L: Well, I've just changed careers. I was a school teacher, but I found it really stressful, so I left and became a sales rep for a publisher.

P: Like most of us then …

2

D = David, C = Carolina

D: So, what do you think about it so far?

C: Not much, to be honest. I haven't really learned anything I didn't already know.

D: I know what you mean. But I did go to a good talk yesterday afternoon. It actually really impressed me and the speaker was really good.

C: What was so good about him?

3

C = Carolina, J = John

C: Hi, John. How's the new job? And what do you think of Rosario?

J: Oh, hi Carolina. Yeah, everything's good. I think I know what I'm doing in the job now and Rosario's great.

C: That's good. I'm glad you like it. Is it very different from your hometown, then?

J: It's really different. It's much bigger than my hometown, Stow. Stow's quite small and there's not that much to do.

C: Is Stow a historic town then?

J: Oh yes. Lots of the buildings are from the eighteenth century.

C: Really?

4

C = Carolina, B = Ben

C: Hey Ben. How was the flight?

B: Oh, it was awful. There was a screaming baby right next to me. And the food was disgusting too as usual.

C: Oh no – poor you. When did you land?

B: Oh, about five o'clock yesterday evening.

C: So how did you get from the airport to the hotel?

B: By taxi.

C: And that was in the rush hour then! What was the traffic like?

B: Pretty bad actually. It took about 40 minutes more than it normally does.

))) 4.6

1

I = interviewers (1 and 2), D = Darren

I1: So where do you see yourself in five years' time?

D: I believe I will have made this hotel chain one of the largest and most profitable in the country. I feel the hotel has the potential to expand globally and that I'm the man with the strategic vision to deliver that.

I2: In a situation where a senior member of your team is not performing to the best of their ability, what would you do?

D: I tell them my concerns and ultimately if they do not perform, they are out. A successful business cannot move on with people like that in their management team.

2

I = interviewers (1, 2 and 3), S = Susan

I1: Hi, Nice to meet you. You found us OK then?

S: Yes, actually I've stayed here before.

I2: Now I feel like we're being judged! When did you stay here?

S: I think it was about three years ago.

I3: Oh, so before our renovation then?

S: Yes, it looks amazing. I love what you've done to the reception and the menu looks fantastic. I think even if I don't get the job, I'll come back again!

I1: Right, yes, the job. OK, let's get down to business. So, what unique skills do you bring to the position?

S: Wherever I've worked, I've been extremely successful. I don't believe I would ever be anything else. By hiring me, you are guaranteeing success for your company.

Unit 5

3

I = interviewers (1, 2 and 3), J = Jenny

I1: What challenges have you faced in your life and how have you overcome them?

J: I was never the strongest academically, but I always try to give my best. From my first job, I realised I was good with people and used this skill to build my career in hospitality. I try to do the same for my staff. I try to help people, especially young people, to identify their strengths and to use these to the best of their ability. It gives me great satisfaction helping others and seeing people realise or achieve their ambitions.

I1: Yes, I try to do the same for my staff. Well, it was a pleasure meeting you today.

J: Thank you for taking the time to meet me. I hope the wedding reception goes well tonight.

I1: I'm sure it will. We might steal your idea for tonight!

I2: I'm already on the case.

I3: Any other ideas, while you're still here?

J: Oh you'll have to hire me to get those.

I1: Thanks again for coming. Enjoy your weekend out in London.

J: I can't wait, I love it here. Have a nice weekend.

◀))) 4.7

I = interviewers (1, 2 and 3)

I1: OK, so shall we work through each of them in turn?

I2: Yes, why not.

I3: So, Darren Tasker. On paper outstanding.

I1: Yes, without doubt the best candidate.

I2: Really? I found him a bit cold and distant.

I1: Yes, but his experience, drive and ambition really gave me a sense that he knew where to take this company.

I2: I think he had more of a sense of where he was going and how he could use us to get there.

I3: Exactly! How long would he be here? Also, whilst he has a clear strategy for the hotel, could he keep the staff happy or the customers for that matter?

I1: True. Well, how about Susan De Costa? A lovely person.

I3: Yes, and very professional in manner and appearance. She's also well qualified and has been successful in business before.

I2: But not quite the same sector. It's very different keeping people happy for an hour or two in comparison to a week or two.

I1: But it is still in the hospitality sector, so it's transferable.

I3: She seems like a confident person.

I2: Borderline arrogant if you ask me.

I3: I know what you mean, there's a fine line between confidence and arrogance. How about Jenny Flynn?

I1: The outstanding interviewee if you ask me.

I2: I thought Darren was the outstanding candidate?

I1: Yes, but Jenny gave the best interview. I think she'd be excellent at managing staff. She really puts herself in her team's position and imagines what they would want and what they'd be good at.

I3: She would also be excellent with customers. As we all know, your contact with guests is limited so when you do meet them you have to make an excellent first impression and she'd certainly do that!

I1: I guess what it comes down to then is which is more important – experience or first impressions?

◀))) 5.1

L = Lars, A = Alain

L: What's the best way to build a business relationship in Argentina?

A: You must take the time to meet people face to face. You can send emails, but talking in person is much more effective.

L: So meetings are an important part of business life?

A: They are. You have to be punctual to meetings, but don't expect people to start talking about work straight away. They talk a lot about football, weekends, holidays – all sorts of things and you should join because they help build the business relationship. You must engage in these and not push it to work topics too quickly.

L: So communication is important in a meeting?

A: Yes, and body language. Eye contact is longer and people stand close together. It's all part of their style, I know in northern Europe we make less eye contact and stand further apart.

L: What about managing in Argentina?

A: Being a manager in Argentina is complex for someone who doesn't understand the culture. The hierarchy is strict, you have to be the boss and show you are in charge, but you should also be friendly with your staff. It's a bit like a parent and child relationship – being very close but also maintaining control.

L: So, social occasions are important?

A: Very, but you shouldn't talk about work too much. Only do it if your host starts the conversation. When we do talk business, we usually do it after the meal, during coffee.

◀))) 5.2

L = Lars, A = Alain

L: OK, some practical questions now. Will I need a visa?

A: You don't have to have one to travel there, but you have to get a visa to work there.

L: OK, what about health care?

A: Health care is very good, but you must get good insurance as it can be expensive.

L: Is life expensive in general?

A: No, it's OK compared to France. You don't have to take a lot of money as it's much cheaper than Paris.

L: What about getting around? Should I buy a car?

A: It depends how much you want to travel. I didn't. The buses are the best way to travel in Argentina. They're great in the city and for long distances. When you want to buy a ticket with a credit card, you mustn't forget your passport.

◀))) 5.3

1

A: We don't have much time. Why don't we go to a café for some fast food?

B: That sounds like a good idea, and it's not expensive.

2

A: It's so crowded in here.

B: How about finding another bar? I know a nice quiet bar just round the corner.

3

A: I'm only in the city for one day. What should I do?

B: If I were you, I'd go to the market in the morning – it's really lively and busy. You can buy fresh snacks. Then go to the beach. Don't be shy – everyone's very sociable and outgoing.

4

A: That was the worst restaurant I've ever been to. Rude staff, plain food and expensive.

B: They often are in tourist areas. Perhaps we should go somewhere more traditional. I really want to try the Feijoada. We might be better off booking though.

))) 5.4

Obviously you need to be an expert in the topic you are talking about, but you also need to think about your audience's knowledge. It's important you consider who you're talking to, their expertise and background. Making your talk too specialised or simplistic will alienate your audience. You also need to make sure you have clear objectives so that the content is organised logically. You need to use clear signposting language to structure your presentation, this is especially important if you have to deliver a long presentation. Regarding technology, you need to consider the appearance of slides if you are using PowerPoint. A good starting point is to use the six by six rule – six bullet points with no more than six words in each line. Also when presenting, be prepared for technology to go wrong and be prepared to present without it. The next two things to consider are related, both body language and delivery are key to a good presentation. Even when the content is detailed and you are clearly knowledgeable, it's easy to perform poorly. By this I mean using pauses, stress and intonation to maintain the audience's interest. The speed of delivery should also not be too slow or too fast. If you speak too quickly, people won't understand you and if you speak too slowly, people just won't pay attention. Effective body language, such as maintaining eye contact and the use of gestures can also help to keep the audience's interest. Lastly, you should obviously look smart and professional. People form very quick impressions about people and your appearance will influence their perception of you.

))) 5.5, 5.6

The key to any successful small enterprise is planning. Detailed planning is key to obtaining funding and investment, whether that's a loan from a bank, investment from other businesses or funds borrowed from family and friends. People will want to know that you know exactly what you're doing, how their money's being used and what the return on their investment is likely to be. Would you be happy to invest in a poorly planned and thought out idea? No, I very much doubt anyone would. So before you even think about telling anyone what your idea is, plan the details carefully.

))) 5.7

Hi, Nick It's Karim. We have a group of twenty new employees coming over for six months from the UK. Could you find someone to deliver a presentation on living and working in Dubai? Thanks.

))) 5.8

N = Nick, K = Karim

N: So, what do you think of the different options?

K: To be honest, I've never seen Mohammed present, but the feedback's very impressive, with lots of good testimonials. In some ways it's good to have someone in the company as well.

N: I know Mohammed well. I saw him present at a sales conference last year.

K: What's he like?

N: He's not very original, it's a little bit death by PowerPoint.

K: And they still liked him?

N: Yes, he's one of the most entertaining and funniest presenters you'll ever see. It's almost like watching a comedian!

K: Well that's good – relax everyone in their new environment. Does he know much about the UK?

N: I'm not sure. Possibly not. How about Chris from the British Society?

K: Well, I'm sure he'd be much more informative. He's experienced moving to a new country and culture. You don't always notice the important things when you know a place well, i.e. your own culture.

N: Yes, but have you seen the photos on their website and the events they run?

K: No. Why?

N: I'm not sure they'll be very culturally sensitive.

K: Hmm, difficult. How about ICT? Very professional looking site and experienced.

N: Also they have experience between the Middle East and the UK.

K: They are very expensive though. Couldn't we do it ourselves?

Unit 6

))) 6.1

1

S = customer service, C = customer

S: Good morning. How can I help?

C: Finally! I've been trying to contact someone all day!

S: Have you tried our website? Most questions can be answered there.

C: Yes, I have tried it and I've sent five emails, but I haven't received a response.

S: Oh, sorry about that. How can I help?

C: I'd like to make an insurance claim. My bike's been stolen.

2

I = IT services, C = customer

I: IT services. How can I help?

C: I've been having problems with my computer all day.

I: What seems to be the problem?

C: It's crashed twice and the screen has frozen three times.

I: Have you tried switching it on and off again?

C: I've done that five times now.

I: OK, I'm going to access your computer remotely. What's your user name and password?

3

M = Mark, T = Tom

M: Hi, is that Tom?

T: Yes it is. Who's calling?

M: Tom, it's Mark here from Eastlight. I still haven't received the information for the training course.

T: Really? How long ago did you request it?

M: I've been waiting for three weeks now and the course starts next week.

T: Really sorry about that. I'll follow it up personally today and get it sent out asap.

))) 6.2

We've changed how we work in many ways. In terms of Internet presence, we've started to use social media such as Facebook and Twitter, especially Twitter, which increased its number of tweets per day very slowly from 2007 to January

2009 to one million. In the next year, it shot up to nearly 50 million per day. It's now a key way to contact our customers. The second change is that we have to work much harder to keep our customers by personalising our services. Customer loyalty for people born before 1929 was high, at just over 55%. This increased gradually to 57% for war babies and then fell slightly for the baby boomers back to 55%. This then decreased to 50% for Generation X and then plummeted to nearly 40% for Generation Y. The last change is that we now do nearly all of our business on the Internet. We have few call centres or shops and do nearly everything online. Our customers expect instant products and instant answers to their questions. Our sales online increased by one million every year for the first three years and then jumped by five million every year after that and now stand at thirteen million per year.

))) 6.3

1

L = Lucy, S = Salvo

L: Hello.

S: Hi, is that Lucy?

L: Yes, how can I help?

S: It's Salvo here. Unfortunately, there's a problem with the order you sent.

L: Hi, Salvo. Sorry to hear that. What's the problem?

S: We ordered 1,000 A4 brochures and 500 A5 brochures, but we've got the opposite.

L: Mm, I'm just looking at your email now and I can see it's our mistake. I'll send out out an extra 500 A4 brochures and you can keep the extra 500 A5 brochures for free.

S: Excellent, thank you, Lucy!

2

M = Marcus, R = Ruben

M: Hello, ISLC Printing. How can I help?

R: Hi, we have a photocopier on hire from you and the paper keeps getting stuck.

M: Do you mean you can't print anything?

R: We can print individual sheets of paper, but nothing in groups. No hole punching or stapling.

M: I think we'll have to send out an engineer. Someone will be with you this afternoon.

R: Great, thank you.

3

M = Mohammed, A = Anastasia

M: About time – I've been waiting for ages!

A: I'm sorry about the delay. How can I help?

M: It's my computer – it keeps crashing.

A: Could you explain when and how?

M: It's every time I access the Internet. I can't use my emails.

A: Have you tried switching it on and off again?

M: Yes, of course I have.

A: Sorry, it does work quite often though. Is your anti-virus software up to date?

M: I'm not sure actually.

A: I think you should check that and then get back to me if it still doesn't work.

M: OK, so I'll have to do all the work myself – great!

))) 6.4

L = Lucy, S = Salvo

L: Hello.

S: Hi, is that Lucy?

L: Yes, how can I help?

S: It's Salvo here. Unfortunately there's a problem with the order you sent.

L: Hi, Salvo. Sorry to hear that. What's the problem?

S: We ordered 1,000 A4 brochures and 500 A5 brochures, but we've got the opposite.

L: Mm, I'm just looking at your email now and I can see it's our mistake. I'll send out an extra 500 A4 brochures and you can keep the extra 500 A5 brochures for free.

S: Excellent, thank you, Lucy!

))) 6.5

M = Monica, L = Lukas

M: This is getting really quite bad. We're getting a bad reputation for service now. Look at the responses to question 5. Five years ago, 90% of people were happy with the outcome of their complaint.

L: Yes, but now it's fallen again. It fell by about 10% every year and now it's fallen by another 20%. It's terrible!

M: I think this last question is the most interesting. The five main things that could be done are:

1 Positive friendly customer service

2 React calmly

3 Make the service more personal

4 Improve staff knowledge

5 Keep better records of complaints.

10% of people all said 1, 2 and 3 – that's worrying – it's basic customer service!

L: 40% said our staff knowledge needs to be improved! That's shocking.

M: And 30% want better records kept. I guess they've been having to repeat themselves all the time.

L: We need to take action!

))) 6.6

Paloma

P = Paloma, R = Ruban, M = Mary

P: Good afternoon, Paloma speaking. How can I help?

R: I bought a computer from you recently that was faulty. You replaced it and now this one has gone wrong as well.

P: Oh, I'm sorry to hear that. Would you like us to replace the computer?

R: No thank you, I'd like a refund, please.

P: Sorry, one minute. I just need to take this call.

R: Sorry, what?!

M: What's happening dear?

R: No idea. I think she just answered her mobile!

P: Sorry about that. What did you say the problem was?

R: The second computer you have sent me has broken. I'd like a ...

P: One minute. What's that Rodrigo? A beer, yeah I'll just deal with this and be with you in a minute. Sorry sir, we're having problems with our computer system.

R: So am I. I want a refund.

P: I'll send you a new PC on Monday. Have a nice weekend.

R: Incredible!

Tomas

T = Tomas, G = Guido

T: Yes.

G: Is that Elba computing?

T: Yes.

G: Who am I speaking to?

T: Tomas.

G: OK. Tomas, I can't access my cloud that you host.

T: Yeah, lots of people are having that problem.

G: So you can solve it easily?

T: No.

G: Right ... so what can I do?

T: You'll just have to wait, my friend.

G: But I need to access my work now.

T: Nothing I can do. Bye.

G: What?! Oi ... idiot!

Unit 7

·))) 7.1

M = Maria, C = Carlos

M: So it's no longer a man's world then.

C: What?

M: Look, according to this we are just going to be human, and not men and women.

C: Ridiculous! Let's see ... Well, some of this is happening, more women are working and getting more powerful jobs, but I don't think that's true.

M: The decline of manufacturing and construction? I agree that people are still going to buy products and need offices and places to live, but I do think people are going to buy different products. The point about Apple is true.

C: I agree. You see it in many products such as perfumes, phones and computers. One thing's for sure though. I'm not going to do flower arranging as a hobby.

M: You might not, but some men will.

C: Hmm, will they? Number three is going to happen, but I don't think that's a feminine value. I think it's going to change because it has to. We can't rely on petrol.

M: True, it probably will happen, but not for a long time. So are you going to have plastic surgery?

C: That's not going to happen.

M: I think it will, but only a few people will do it. I don't think five is going to happen.

C: Really? Lots of people I know have become vegan and vegetarian.

M: Yes, but ninety per cent of any menu is still meat or fish. People are going to eat meat for a long time yet.

C: Maybe, but people will start to eat more vegetarian meals. It might not be for the environment, but it is cheaper and healthier.

·))) 7.2

1

S = Simon, D = Diane

S: So moving on to item number five on the agenda. Diane, did you circulate this before?

D: No, sorry I forgot, here it is.

S: OK, well we're not going to be able to read and discuss it now. Please make sure you remember to send agenda items before the meeting.

D: Sorry, I'll give you a quick summary.

2

N = Nikolaou, I = Ilke

N: Is Hazal not here today?

I: She's here – I saw her earlier.

N: Any idea where she is now?

I: She must have forgotten.

N: I sent a meeting invite. This is ridiculous! Can you go and get her, please?

3

F = Fehim, R = Rosa

F: Sorry ... um, where was I?

R: You were talking about sales targets.

F: That's right ... So this month's sales targets. No, sorry, I've spoken about those already. Um, so next month's ...

R: ... sales targets.

F: Yes, sorry ...

·))) 7.3

F = Fehim, R = Rosa

F: Have you seen the staff development week – Working Smarter?

R: I have. What do you think you're going to go to?

F: Well, I can't go to the session on Tuesday afternoon on five tips for managing your time – I'm too busy!

R: What are you doing?

F: I'm meeting a customer at 2.00 and then I'm working with Simon on a new project from 3.00 to 5.00.

R: Typical! He always complains about our time management!

F: I'm going to go to the memory and concentration session though.

R: When does that start?

F: I'm not sure. I can't remember. I think it starts at 9.00 on Wednesday.

R: Are you attending the healthy eating session on Thursday?

F: No I'm having lunch with Diane at 1.00. We're going out for a pizza.

R: You're not going to much then, are you!

F: Well, I would go to the session on relaxation, but it finishes too late for me.

·))) 7.4

1 I hate how many emails I get. I think I can just delete ninety per cent of the emails I get. You can always tell when some people aren't busy because they start 'work' conversations about nothing.

2 I hate how hard it is to focus again after getting an email. It might only take twenty seconds to read, but it often takes me another five minutes to focus on what I was doing.

3 I hate how I can't get away from email. My emails come to my i-phone, my instant messenger and even my TV. I just can't get away from it – ever!

4 I can't stand poor subject lines or people not updating them. Some just don't make it very clear what the message is about and some people just never update them. Three weeks later, the subject line for the same conversation still says 'urgent'.

5 It really annoys me when people can't get to the point. Five paragraphs and 300 words to tell me one or two small pieces of information. Come on!

6 It drives me crazy when people put 'important' and it's not. People can only do that so many times when it's not important and then I'll just delete their emails instantly.

7 It really irritates me when people don't check for mistakes. Their, there or they're. Affect, effect. Your, you're. No one seems to know the difference.

·))) 7.5

S = Karl, S = Sofia

K: It's exciting news, isn't it?

S: I know. I might be able to use my Arabic lessons.

K: Ha ha! Well, we could travel to some interesting places and, if things go well, there might be opportunities for promotion.

S: True, but it's not going to be easy.

K: Why not?

S: Have you not thought about the logistics?

K: What do you mean?

S: Well, the UAE is two hours ahead, which is not too much of a problem, but Malaysia is seven hours ahead.

K: Hmm, but many countries do work with such time zone differences, so it can't be that hard.

S: Well, maybe not, but then there are also the different weekends everyone will have.

K: Really? Obviously we're Saturday and Sunday, but what do they take in the UAE and Malaysia?

S: In Malaysia, it's Thursday and Friday, because the company are based in the North. In the UAE, it's Friday and Saturday.

K: OK. Interesting!

))) 7.6

K = Karl, S = Scott

K: Hi, Scott. Have you got in touch with Svetlana and Ahad yet?

S: I was just going to send an email now.

K: Scott, you can't send a mail like that!

S: Why not? It's friendly and chatty.

K: Yes, but you hardly know them and look how formal their emails are!

S: How should I word it then?

K: Change it to 'Dear Svetlana and Ahad'. Then start with 'I'm afraid that time would not be possible'. Then change the second line to 'Unfortunately, I'm unable to be in the office by 8.00 a.m. on a Monday morning' and then the last line to 'Could we possibly consider an alternative?'

S: That basically says the same thing!

K: Yes, but it's more formal. Come on, you're not on Facebook now! Make sure you add 'Kind regards' as well.

S: OK.

))) 7.7

Sv = Svetlana, A = Ahad, Sc = Scott

Sv: This is crazy. Scott, we'll work for about five hours at the same time for four days a week and Ahad, we'll work for about four hours at the same time for four days a week.

A: Yes and then Scott, we only work for one hour a day at the same time for three days a week.

Sc: This is going to be challenging to co-ordinate. Basically the only days we work that are the same are Monday, Tuesday and Wednesday.

Sv: So all deadlines we set ourselves have to be on a Monday, Tuesday or Wednesday. We can't have it any other day of the week.

Sc: It would be better for me if deadlines are not Monday. Monday is the second or third day of the week for you, but the first for me.

A: OK, let's say all deadlines are Tuesday or Wednesday.

Sv: Can we also have rules about emails? Let's not send emails at the weekend.

Sc: But we can't do that – between us the weekend lasts four days. Let's say no emails on Friday and Saturday.

A: Why Friday and Saturday?

Sc: On both days at least two of us won't be at work so we'll just be filling up each other's inboxes.

Sv: Sounds like a good idea to me.

A: What about conference calls? It's 7.00 p.m. on Wednesday night here. Remember that's like a Thursday or Friday night for you guys!

Sc: True! Sorry, Ahad.

A: It's fine, but I'd prefer not to make it a regular event.

Sv: Scott, could you maybe take part in conference calls early in the morning?

Sc: Sure. Just not Monday, please!

Sv: Well, shall we say conference calls take place on Tuesday and Wednesday mornings between 8.00 a.m. and 10.00 a.m. German time?

A: That works well for me.

Sc: Me too. Right, let's call it a day – enjoy your weekend, Ahad.

Unit 8

))) 8.1

M = manager, D = David

M: So David, you're happy with the terms of the contract?

D: Yes, mostly. Obviously if I move here, I'll need to buy a new house.

M: Oh, we can help with that, no problem. We have lots of houses we use for new players.

D: My wife has seen a house she really wants. If the club helps me buy it, I'll be really happy.

M: You want the club to buy you a house?

D: Yes, kind of like a bonus.

M: Unfortunately that wouldn't be possible. If you want, the club will lend you the money. You'll have to pay it back later.

D: Great, that's a deal. Oh, one other thing. I'd like a $250,000 personal business account.

M: Right … why?

D: Oh, to pay for things like a masseur and horse-riding lessons.

M: Why, are they business expenses?

D: Well, if you buy me, you buy my image. My wife is part of that image.

M: So these expenses are for your wife? Well, if we agree, we'll need you to sign the contract today.

D: Where do I sign?

))) 8.2

M = manager, A = agent

M: So, are there any other terms we need to agree to get the player to sign?

A: Just a couple of minor points. Now, my client is obviously leaving his family in another country to come here.

M: Yes, we know, but we're sure he'll adapt well if we provide language lessons and a translator to help.

A: That's excellent, but it will also help if you allow eight first-class tickets between Japan and Chicago every year for his family.

M: Sorry, but I think he'll make enough money from his contract to pay for these flights!

A: I'm sorry, but the bottom line is he needs to know these are paid for. If he does know this, he'll feel happy that his family can come regularly.

M: If we pay for them, will he sign the deal?

A: Yes. Well, if you pay for and arrange the family visa expenses, this will also help him to feel happy.

M: Sorry, but this is getting ridiculous. Do they want accommodation and food as well?

A: I'm sorry, but if you don't meet these terms, he won't sign.

M: Shouldn't we spend a little more time looking for a compromise?

A: Sorry, no. Pay the money or no deal.

M = Mark, D = Daphne

M: What I propose is we move on to negotiate on price.
D: What do you have in mind?
M: If we increased the order, could you reduce the price by 40 per cent?
D: Well, it would have to be a big increase.
M: We could increase the order to 10,000 items.
D: Let me just check I understand you correctly. You want a 40 per cent discount for a twenty per cent increase in the order.
M: Bear in mind this is a first order. If the product sells well, we might increase our order next time.
D: Would you be willing to accept a compromise? Say a 30% discount?
M: I'm afraid not, perhaps a slightly higher discount.
D: 35%?
M: That would be difficult for us. Please remember the potential size of future orders here. We are the largest retailer in the sector.
D: I know and I really want to work with you, but at the moment, we don't see this as a viable option. We would make a loss at that price.
M: That's our final offer I'm afraid.
D: Then I'm sorry, we don't have a deal.

·))) 8.4

E = Eleni, T = Tayo

E: So you've had a successful year with us, Tayo, and we're very happy with your progress. Is there anything you'd like to discuss with us?
T: Yes, I'd like to discuss my salary. I'd like to ask for an increase.
E: OK, I'm sure there's something we can do. What did you have in mind?
T: I'd like a $10,000 a year increase.
E: That's a twenty per cent increase! I don't think we could do that. Well, actually one option would be to make it part of a bonus package.
T: So if I understand you correctly, you would give me a $10,000 increase, but some would be bonus? What percentage would be bonus?
E: Twenty per cent would be salary related and 80 per cent bonus related.
T: Sorry, that's just too much on bonuses. What if I don't do well?
E: Well, that's kind of the point, Tayo. You've done well, but not that well to ask for such a big rise! What if we offered you an alternative?
T: How about 80:20 the other way?
E: I'm afraid we could only accept this on one condition, that we reduce your commission rate from 10% to 8%.
T: But that would be a pay cut!
E: Not if you perform well.
T: But none of this is what I asked for!
E: No Tayo, it's called negotiation. Go away and think about it and get back to me.

·))) 8.5

Sales manager

We need ten cars in total. Eight of them are used by sales representatives across the country and two are used by sales representatives here in the city. So all are used for sales, but two need to be city cars. It's important that they all have good boot space as we carry a lot of things with us. It's obviously great if they have inbuilt satnav as we spend a lot of time on the road. We also need to be in constant touch so Bluetooth is a must.

Senior management executive

We need six cars for senior management. We don't use the cars a lot. They are mainly for getting to and from work. A lot of us do take clients out to lunch though, so they should look good. It's useful to have cruise control and for the interior to look smart with things like leather seats. The company is generally quite green so things like the miles per gallon are important to match the company image.

Car pool manager

We keep ten cars for pool use and they can be used by anyone in the company. They are for customer visits, travel on training courses, couriering goods – lots of uses really. So many people use them that they have to have adjustable seats. Also it's difficult to predict the mileage, so they need to be efficient and cheap to run with low insurance and servicing costs.

Unit 9

·))) 9.1

Laura

Eventually when I did find it, the meeting was a disaster. I was so late it made me really stressed. Even though I had planned exactly what I wanted to say, I forgot so many things. I think they thought I was really unprepared and not very professional.

Vera

I tried to contact the customer to tell them about the breakdown and delay later that evening. When I did, I realised I had mislaid their contact details. I wasn't too worried because I had their email address in the predictive text of my emails. Unfortunately, I mistyped their email address and sent it to the wrong person. It was similar to another one in my address book and I had clicked on that instead.

Giorgios

My mistyping of lots of the figures made it look like I didn't know what I was doing. Some people thought I had overestimated how long the project would take and that eight weeks was too long. I hadn't miscalculated; I had simply mistyped.

·))) 9.2

1

I was driving to work when I had an accident. I had never had an accident before. It was completely the other driver's fault – he was using his phone when he crashed into me.

2

I was walking down the corridor when I slipped and fell over. Someone had dropped a drink and not cleaned it up. I had had a bad back for a week, but fell and hurt my leg as well

3

I was speaking on the phone all morning on a conference call. My colleague had bought a coffee for me and I hadn't seen them put it down. I knocked it all over my computer.

·))) 9.3

1

A: ... so what we need to do ... hello, hello! Oh bother! ... Sorry about that. I'm not sure what happened.
B: Don't worry about it.
A: So, as I was saying ...

2

C: Hi, I placed an order with your company, but what I've received isn't the thing I ordered.

D: Sorry about that. It must have been mixed up with another order. I'll arrange for a replacement to be sent.

C: When can I expect it to arrive?

D: I'll courier it for first thing tomorrow. Please accept our apologies. I hope it hasn't caused too much inconvenience.

C: That's fine, thank you.

3

E: Hi, I'm afraid I bought the wrong size jumper. I had wanted a medium, but bought small. Could I change it?

F: No problem. We can just replace it.

E: That's great.

F: I think it must have been on the wrong hanger. Here you are.

E: Great. Thank you.

4

G: Hi, excuse me. I ordered the roast beef, not the roast lamb.

H: Oh, sorry, I'll take it back and get you the beef. … Here you are. Please accept our apologies. There'll be no charge for your meal.

⁙)) 9.4

Sorry, could I just interrupt for a moment?
Sorry. I didn't see you there.
Sorry? What did you say?

⁙)) 9.5

J = Julia, M = Mateo

J: Julia Pool speaking, how can I help?

M: Hi Julia, it's Mateo from Alto Coffee.

J: Oh hi. I was planning to call you today. I'm really sorry about the mistake with your order.

M: It did cost us a lot of sales on the day and I think future days. When you lose a regular customer, then you lose a lot of future purchases.

J: I know. I'm really sorry. We think the problem is with the delivery company we used.

M: Right. Well, that's not really my problem I'm afraid.

J: I know.

M: I have to say I'm afraid we might change suppliers because of this. We have had a number of issues with supply and want it improved.

J: Sorry to hear that. Could I perhaps meet you to discuss the issue?

M: Sure, email me with some dates and we'll see what we can do.

Unit 10

⁙)) 10.1

We've tried a number of ideas to make our company greener. We wanted to save money and reduce our carbon footprint. Many of our employees now car share and we have about 20% fewer cars on site every day. We've started an energy monitor to show how much energy each department is using and how much they've saved in the last month – just simple things like turning off lights, computers, machines, etc. It's cut our energy use by 15% and saved us thousands of pounds. We tried a bike scheme, but our company is too far out of town for most people so it wasn't very successful. One unusual one we tried was that we said employees could grow fruit and vegetables on our land. They donate 20% of the food to the work canteen and 80% they can take home. It only saves a small amount of energy, but it has been great for team-building.

⁙)) 10.2

1 The farm's produce is sold at local markets.
  The goods on sale are produced or processed directly at the shop.

2 The ceramics have many different uses.
  It is thin, round and crisp so that it can be kept and used for long periods.

3 Many local products are sold in separate shops and not big stores.
  While many Italian brands have separated from their Italian roots, even today Gucci is strongly linked to Italy's Tuscan region.

4 Some people object to so many goods being imported.
  They are still popular objects to collect, use or give as a present today.

5 They presented her with a Gucci bag.
  They are still popular objects to collect, use or give as a present today.

⁙)) 10.3

M = manager, Z = Zlatan

M: So Zlatan, could you fill us in on the details of the survey?

Z: Certainly. Well, just to give you some background first. According to many surveys, the market for green goods is up 180%.

M: That's impressive growth. How does this compare to previous years?

Z: The market has been growing steadily, but this is by far the biggest growth.

M: And what percentage of our sales is it now?

Z: Roughly speaking, it's now 24% of our sales.

M: Really? Can we look at the figures for overall sales?

Z: The end result is the sales are worth $500 million.

M: There's clearly a growing desire for this type of product.

Z: Yes, the main trend is for growth.

M: And we have kept pace with this.

Z: Yes, we've been expanding our product range on a monthly basis by around 5%.

M: What's that in terms of the growth of our product range?

Z: Well, it's approximately 110 new products every month.

M: OK, let's look at some of the trends in our product range …

⁙)) 10.4

S = Sienna, M = Monty

S: So, Monty could you fill us in on the results from the staff survey?

M: The overriding trend is that employees believe that a lot can be done.

S: Excellent. Can we look at the figures for each one?

M: 90% think that there's too much paper wasted and that more should be digital.

S: Too much paper waste? How does this compare to other waste?

M: Well, it's much higher, but 20% thought that too much non-work waste is produced from drinks and vending machines.

S: That's an unusual one. Not sure what we can do about that. How do people feel about our recycling?

M: 50% felt that not enough waste is recycled. A lot of other responses were related to energy.

S: Such as …?

M: 75% think the heating's left on too long and 55% think too much heat is lost in the building. A further 30% think too much energy's used when lights are left on.

S: So what's that in terms of actual numbers?

M: Well, that's as many as 400 employees. The bottom line is most people think more can be done.

S: OK, any other factors?

M: Well, 15% think too many people drive to work and all the others were below 10%.

 **Richmond**

58 St Aldates
Oxford
OX1 1ST
United Kingdom

© 2013, Santillana Educación, S.L. / Richmond
Publisher: Ruth Goodman
Editor(s): Anna Gunn, David Cole-Powney, Stephanie Parker
Digital Publisher: Luke Baxter
Design Manager: Lorna Heaslip
Cover Illustration & Design: This Ain't Rock'n'Roll
Design & Layout: Oliver Hutton/www.zoomdesigns.co.uk
Picture Editors: Helen Reilly/www.arnosdesign.co.uk, Magdalena Mayo
Art Coordinator: Dave Kuzmicki

ISBN: 978-84-668-1405-8

First edition: 2013

Printed in Spain
D.L. M-5560-2013

No unauthorised photocopying

Publisher acknowledgements:
The Publisher would like to thank all those who have given their kind permission to reproduce material for this book:

Texts:
p4 Extract from 'A Day in the Life of a Budding Supermodel' from reuters.com, by Sarah Marsh. Reprinted by permission. All rights reserved. Republication or redistribution of Thomson Reuters content, including by framing or similar means, is expressly prohibited without the prior written consent of Thomson Reuters. Thomson Reuters and its logo are registered trademarks or trademarks of the Thomson Reuters group of companies around the world. ©Thomson Reuters 2008. Thomson Reuters journalists are subject to an Editorial Handbook which requires fair presentation and disclosure of relevant interests.
p5 Track 1.1 Extract from 'Feared by pedestrians, despised by cabbies: the life and hard times of a London courier' by Matthew Sparkes. Guardian News & Media Ltd ©2009. Reprinted by permission.
p6 Extract from 'Management: An Introduction', David Boddy and Steve Paton, Pearson Education Limited ©2011. Reprinted by permission.
p28 Extract from 'My high-flying City job was not worth a life of misery' by Anuska Asthana. Guardian News & Media Ltd ©2006. Reprinted by permission.
p60 Extract from 'Use Twitter to Get Free Stuff by Complaining', originally published at www.dailytekk.com. Reprinted by permission of DailyTekk founder Chris O'Connell.
p74 Extract from 'What would you do if you could name your own salary?' by Jim Hopkinson, originally published at http://www.salary.com/name-your-own-salary. Reprinted by permission.
p76 Extract from 'How to negotiate with an Indian' by Bob Compton, published at http://www.fourhourworkweek.com/blog/2007/12/11/how-to-negotiate-like-an-indian-7-rules/. Reprinted by permission of Dave Compton.
p84 Extracts from 'Saying sorry' by Peter M. Sandman, originally published at http://www.psandman.com/col/sorry.htm. Reprinted by permission.
p88 Extracts from 'Santropol Roulant: A Leaner, Greener Meals on Wheels', originally published on Worldwatch Institute's Nourishing the Planet blog (http://blogs.worldwatch.org/nourishingtheplanet/blog). Reprinted by permission of Danielle Nierenberg.

p88 Extract from 'An Effort to Bury a Throwaway Culture One Repair at a Time', article by Sally McGrane. From The New York Times, 9th May 2012 ©2012 The New York Times. Reprinted by permission.
p89 Extracts from 'Meet Jayride, Anthill 2011 Cool Company Award Winner [Social Capitalist Category]', published at http://anthillonline.com. Reprinted by permission of James Tuckerman.
p92 Extracts from 'Quick Pulse: Green Buying – An Exploration of "Green" Consumer Trends' by Euromonitor International, originally published at http://blog.euromonitor.com/2012/03/quick-pulse-green-buying-an-exploration-of-green-consumer-trends.html. Reprinted by permission.

Illustrations:
Acute Graphics, Richard Allen (Eye Candy Illustration), Francis Blake (Three-In-A-Box).

Photographs:
Arnos Design Ltd; CES, Polly Courtney, FaithPopcorn.com; Oliver Hutton, Mayang.com, Oticon, Plainpicture, Press Association, Random House, Repaircafe.org; Rex Features Ltd, Riverfood Organic, Peter Sandman.

ALAMY/H.Mark Weldman Photography, Fancy, Image Source, Gareth Byrne, Richard Levine, Wayne Tippets, Jeff Greenberg, Caro, Blend Images, Greg Balfour Evans, Oleksiy Maksymenko Photography, Photo Alto, Drive Images, Rachel Husband, Travelling Light, Steve Stock, Stanley Hare, Alex Segre; **CORBIS**/Atlantide Phototravel, Juice Images, Tim Pannell, Vincent Hazat, Andrew Holbrooke, Bettman, Radius Images, Jim Craigmyle, Tetra Images, Eric Audras/Photo Alto, Ocean, Westend 61, Jon Feingersh/Blend Imagess, Tim Pannell, Stock4B, Laura Doss, Uli Wiesmeier, Neil Guegan, Larry Dale Gordon, Image Source, Randy Faris, Jason Butcher/Cultura, Deborah Feingold, Isaac Lane Koval, Walter Bibikow/JAI, Buero Monaco/Zefa, Whisson/Jordan, Tetra Images, Lew Robertson, KMSS, Simon Potter, Beau Lark, Paul Burns, James Leynse, Spaces images, Jarratt; **GETTY IMAGES, SPAIN**/ Jeremy Woodhouse, Lars Ruecker, Ryan McVay, Randy Brooke, Kirsten Sinclair, Blend Images, OJO Images/Chris Ryan, LWA, David Lees, Fuse, Nikada, Thomas Barwick, Stewart Cohen, Paul Bradbury, Jasper James, Peter Adams, Greg Elms, Bloomberg, Image Source, Flying Colours Ltd, John Lund/Marc Romanelli, V Stock LLC, Peter Dazeley, Peter Cade, David & Les Jacobs, Bambu Productions, Aping Visions, General Photographic agency, Cultura, SelectStock, Richard 1'Anson, Arabian eye, Bloomberg, Gary Conner, Photodisc, David Lees, I Love Images, Ryan McVay, Jose Luis Pelaez Inc, Brian Mc Entire, Monty Rakusen, Johnny Haglund, Adam Gault, Vincenzo Lombardo, Diane Cook & Len Jenshel, Peathegee Inc, Bloomberg, Bernie de Chant, Loreto Cantero López, Randy Wells, Bloomimage; **ISTOCKPHOTO**/TOMML, STEEX, Logorilla, mbbirdy, Yuri Arcurs, ismet, Dimos, laflor, drbimages, adventtr, sematadesign,iconeer; **THINKSTOCK**/Purestock, Jupiter Images, Creatas, Ingram Publishing, TongRo Images, Ryan McVay, Hemera, Siri Stafford, George Doyle, Michael Blann, NA, Top Photo Group, Mike Powell, FogStock,

The Publisher would like to thank the following reviewers for their invaluable feedback on @work. We extend our thanks to the many other teachers and students around the world whose input has helped us to develop the materials.

Reviewers:
Angela Lilley, The Open University, Oxford, United Kingdom; Manuel Hidalgo Iglesias, QUILL Language Learning, Mexico City, Mexico; Marion Grussendorf, ACADIA GmbH, Cologne, Germany; Paulo Henrique Vaz Lopes, Cultura Inglesa Belo Horizonte, Brazil; Radmila Petrova Kaisheva & Anna Rumenova Boyadzhieva-Moskova, University of National and World Economy, Sofia, Bulgaria; Andrew Archer, Independent Publishers International, Tokyo, Japan

Every effort has been made to trace the holders of copyright before publication. The Publisher will be pleased to rectify any errors or omissions at the earliest opportunity.